# HERO
## DINNERS

# HERO DINNERS

## COMPLETE ONE-PAN MEALS THAT SAVE THE DAY

### MARGE PERRY
### and DAVID BONOM

WILLIAM MORROW
*An Imprint of HarperCollinsPublishers*

HarperCollins books may be purchased for educational,
business, or sales promotional use. For information, please
email the Special Markets Department at
SPsales@harpercollins.com.

FIRST EDITION

DESIGNED BY RENATA DE OLIVEIRA

PHOTOGRAPHY BY MARGE PERRY,
EXCEPT FOR PHOTOGRAPH ON PAGE 5 BY MATT TAYLOR-GROSS

SLATE BACKGROUND BY
IMAGINE PHOTOGRAPHER/SHUTTERSTOCK

Library of Congress Cataloging-in-Publication Data
has been applied for.

ISBN 978-0-06-285606-7

19 20 21 22 23  LSC  10 9 8 7 6 5 4 3 2 1

## TO RACHEL AND ZAK,

OUR CAPTIVE AND MOSTLY WILLING TASTERS
FOR SO MANY YEARS; WE TAUGHT YOU MANNERS
AND MORALS AND YOU NOURISH OUR LIVES.
WE'VE ALWAYS KNOWN WE GOT THE BETTER END
OF THE DEAL. —MOM AND EBO

## TO DAD,

WITH DEEP APPRECIATION FOR OUR EPIC ADVENTURES,
YOUR UNWAVERING BELIEF IN ME, AND ALL THE
GREAT HAND-ME-DOWN LENSES. THERE'S NO ONE
WITH WHOM I'D RATHER CRAWL UNDER THE BACK
FENCE OF THE TAJ MAHAL. —MARGE

## TO MY BROTHER FRANK,

THE ONLY PERSON WHO WAS MORE EXCITED
I WAS GOING INTO THE FOOD WORLD THAN I WAS.
THANKS, FRANK, FOR ALWAYS POURING THE
VERY BEST. —DAVID

# CONTENTS

# INTRODUCTION

We cook all day for work. It's our dream job; not only do we create recipes for magazines, websites, and corporations, we get to do it together. And you should see our counters at the end of the day—they're laden with food! But, as crazy as it sounds, when 6 p.m. rolls around, we often look at each other and say, "What do you want to do about dinner?"

Sure, we've been cooking for eight straight hours—and the result might be half a dozen cakes and variations of sticky buns, fifteen kinds of ice pops, or hamburgers that have sat under photography lights for four hours. But no dinner.

We're tired and hungry and yes—cooked out. As much as we love what we do, there are times when evening comes and the last thing we want to think about is dirtying more pots and pans. (Seriously: we've been washing dishes *all day*.) We want a great meal that takes almost no effort to prepare—and even less effort to clean up. And we don't want takeout.

Our solution lies with the humble sheet pan and its kitchen cabinet bestie, the skillet. These two ordinary pieces of cookware transform everyday ingredients into hero dinners.

We all need hero dinners: meals made from real, whole ingredients that practically cook themselves. A hero dinner swoops in and saves the day. Not only is it a meal you throw together with confidence and ease, you can sit down to dinner and truly relax, knowing there's only one pan to clean.

That's why we created this book. We don't want the hour leading up to dinner to be about getting out a bunch of pans, matching flavors and textures of several side dishes, and figuring out timing. At the end of the day, we just don't want to think that hard. We want to enjoy a lovely, wholesome homemade meal—and we want the respite of dinnertime to be more than a brief interlude before we have to (once again) clean up.

Hero dinners get a lot of their super power from the fact that they are made in just one sheet pan or skillet. But you can't just throw any old ingredients in a pan and have them come out tasting great and all cooked to the right degree of doneness. You need the right simple techniques and combination of flavors and textures to magically elevate commonplace ingredients into delicious complete meals.

Okay, so maybe it isn't really magic—but there is something awe-inspiring about the deeply savory, gorgeously browned chicken with crisp-tender Brussels sprouts and starchy purple potatoes we made in one skillet—and with only about fifteen minutes of prep time. And while it may not *technically* be considered magic, we don't know what else to call our incredibly satisfying meal—all made on one sheet pan—of tender, juicy pork chops topped with savory Italian salsa verde and accompanied by sweet potatoes and garlicky broccoli rabe.

Sometimes the "magic" lies in respecting the inherently good flavors of whole ingredients. Like when you roast red snapper fillets that are sprinkled with fresh herbs and lemon zest and nestled next to baby new potatoes and a handful of cherry tomatoes. In half an hour, you sit down to tender, mild snapper with a pop of bright intensity from the roasted tomatoes and golden-crusted potatoes. The great thing about this dinner—besides that it is more delicious and healthful than something this easy has a right to be—is that after you make it once, you won't need a recipe again. You own this now: you won't even have to think about how to make it the next time.

Other times, we use simple condiments or seasoning to take the meal to the next level. Whether it is a sauce, spice rub, or myriad other robustly flavorful ingredients, we think of these as the fairy dust that transforms the ordinary into the extraordinary—with very little additional work, of course.

We're also big fans of blender sauces, which can be as varied as the sunset orange ajvar sauce (page 172) made with eggplant and peppers, umami-rich Italian salsa verde (page 127), or creamy Peruvian ají verde (page 36), made with cilantro, jalapeño, and mayonnaise. We also use condiments from around the world, including spicy harissa sauce, which is available in more and more grocery stores. Harissa invigorates chicken with its exotic heat—and all we do is spread a little over the surface. It's delicious and healthful and requires almost no work to impart loads of flavor.

Of course, the interpretation of "healthy" when it comes to food is both everchanging and highly personal. We use the knowledge we have garnered from writing about nutrition and developing recipes for magazines like *Cooking Light*, *EatingWell*, *Self*, and *Fitness* and a wide range of bestselling diet cookbooks and health-focused companies. While some folks are willing to live on juice, eat like cavemen, or give up entire food groups (even chocolate!) in the name of

healthy eating, we believe a diet based on fewer processed foods, more vegetables, and moderate amounts of intensely flavorful ingredients is a realistic, happy way to cook and eat—as long as the food is truly satisfying.

Nearly everyone agrees that the use of natural, clean ingredients is best. It is an essential part of our cooking style and philosophy that our recipes rely on the flavors and textures of whole and minimally processed foods. Smart, simple techniques maximize the impact of every ingredient, and the results are meals you can feel good about eating and feeding to your family. But for the record: we recognize the important role some processed foods can have in getting a home-cooked meal on the table. We believe using the occasional processed product is not an issue—especially if it makes the difference between ordering in and cooking. The problem arises when every meal relies on foods made with chemical preservatives, loads of salt, and crazy amounts of added sugars.

We created all these recipes to satisfy our day-to-day weeknight needs, but we often end up serving them to company. While we love preparing elaborate feasts for friends—it's one of the reasons we both ended up cooking for a living—it just isn't always practical. With a booming business and too little time on our hands, sometimes it's really nice to be able to tell friends to come on over, even on a Friday night. So while most of these recipes are weeknight friendly (there are a handful of slow-cooking Sunday supper meals, too), a slew of them are also great for gatherings (see Recipes by Category, page 270).

No matter when or to whom we serve it, a hero dinner is our reward at the end of the day. It is the time for us to relax and talk, vent, laugh: to share the pleasure of a great meal that nourishes our bodies and spirits.

## A HERO DINNER HAS TO EARN ITS MONIKER! TO QUALIFY, IT:

- Cooks entirely in one sheet pan or a skillet.

- Always includes protein and at least one vegetable and/or starch (and often both).

- Is made from wholesome, minimally processed ingredients.

- Doesn't require obscure ingredients—but definitely may include accessible new ones.

- And, maybe most important of all, a hero dinner is satisfying and delicious—it's a meal we want to eat again (and again).

# THE HERO DINNER GUIDEBOOK
## (OR, HOW TO BECOME A HERO-DINNER MAKER)

Over the years, we have listened to, spoken with, and learned from the thousands of home cooks we have taught at the Institute of Culinary Education in New York City. We are enormously grateful to all our students who shared their concerns, fears, frustrations, and misunderstandings—as well as their interest and real desire to learn—about getting dinner on the table.

Over and over again, we hear that timing—that is, getting all the elements of a meal done at the same time—is the most stressful part of cooking. With hero dinners, you don't have to worry about timing—all the elements are timed out for you within one recipe.

Knowing when food is cooked to the right degree of doneness is another big concern. We give you tangible ways to test for doneness in every recipe. Using visual cues in the recipe as your guide, and often an instant-read meat thermometer as well, is key to cooking food enough—but not too much! (More on both below.)

Menu planning—especially when life is pulling you in ten different directions—can be a challenge. Again, this book takes care of that: one recipe *is* your entire meal! There's no need to figure out what goes with what—the meal is planned. (We're all for your making substitutions if you want to, though.)

We also learned from students, friends, and family that there are nuances to the way recipes are written that are easy to miss. We wrote these recipes with the singular goal of ensuring your success when you follow them. We want you to love every meal you make, and for you not to have to stress or wonder "Is that what this means?" To that end, we want to fill you in on a few important points about following recipes. But before we do, a PSA of sorts: *reading the recipe all the way through before you start to cook really can make a difference—and ultimately save you time.*

## THE SECRETS TO READING AND FOLLOWING A RECIPE

We've been writing recipes for magazines and cookbooks for years, and we can say with 100 percent certainty that every publication (and person) has its own style. Despite that, there are some behind-the-scenes conventions you should be aware of. They can help you prepare food more efficiently and make your meals more delicious.

### TIME IS A GUIDELINE, NOT A COMMAND.

Your stove, oven, and pans are different from ours, and will therefore conduct heat differently. That's why we try to always give you a visual cue to go by. Say you are cooking chicken thighs in a skillet. We might write, "Cook until the underside is well browned, 4 to 5 minutes." Your goal is to brown the chicken, not to cook it for a certain amount of time. If it takes you 6—or even 7—minutes to get it browned, so be it.

### THE DIFFERENCE BETWEEN A LIQUID MEASURING CUP AND A DRY MEASURING CUP MATTERS.

One cup in a liquid measure is 8 fluid ounces, but you sure aren't going to fit 8 ounces of potato chips in a 1-cup dry measure. Sometimes 1 cup of fluid ounces measures the same as 1 dry cup—but sometimes it doesn't. Use the liquid measure for anything you can pour and the dry measure when it is about how much space (volume) something takes up. (Sour cream, for example, is too thick to pour, so you measure it in the dry cup.) Choose the right tool for the job—it can make a difference.

### THE LIST OF INGREDIENTS AT THE BEGINNING OF EVERY RECIPE IS ACTUALLY YOUR FIRST SET OF DIRECTIONS.

Before you start cooking, make your ingredients look the way they are described in that list. If the ingredient reads "1 cup cherry tomatoes, halved," get them washed and cut in half before you start cooking. You don't want to be in the midst of cooking (for example) a delicate piece of fish and realize you have to stop to cut things up—your fish will get overcooked! We have a bunch of very inexpensive little stackable glass bowls that we use for our readied, measured ingredients. We just stick them in the dishwasher as we go. We promise this is a time—and dinner—saver, and it keeps you organized.

### THERE'S A VERY BIG, VERY IMPORTANT DIFFERENCE BETWEEN "½ CUP CHOPPED PARSLEY" AND "½ CUP PARSLEY, CHOPPED."

When you measure *½ cup chopped parsley*, you are, quite simply, measuring chopped parsley. When you measure *½ cup parsley, chopped*, the comma tells you there are two steps to take: the first is to measure the parsley and the second is to chop it. The difference between the two can be two to three times the volume! This rule applies to all ingredients, but the difference in volume can range greatly: sometimes it barely matters and other times it could ruin your dinner.

## SUPER POWER TOOLS

In cooking, as with so much in life, having the right tools helps enormously. Wonder Woman has her Lasso of Truth and Spiderman his webs. Fortunately, you don't need anything that fancy or special to make hero dinners. In fact, you probably already have the tools it takes.

## SHEET PAN

It is essential that the sheet pan have a low (1-inch) rim all the way around—and that it not be flimsy. (We'll never forget the time we did a demo with disposable aluminum sheet pans, which bent under the weight of the food and sent hot liquid pouring into the bottom of the oven, where it scorched.) But that doesn't mean you need to spend a lot of money to get exactly what you need. In fact, the sheet pans we used to create and test the recipes in this book ranged from $10 to $21. We used an 11 x 17-inch nonstick and a classic commercial-style 13 x 18-inch sheet pan.

We put both pans through vigorous testing, using them more times in an average week than most home cooks will do in a month (or two!). There is no doubt that our nonstick sheet pan is easier to clean and still looks good after months of intense cooking. On the other hand, the commercial sheet pan is less expensive and slightly larger. But after a couple of uses, we can't get it clean without Herculean effort. So we decided to give up and like the patina (the brown baked-in mess in the corners and up the sides that seems to spread a little with every use). We replace the commercial sheet pans when they get too grubby looking. (Our nonstick pan, on the other hand, won't need replacing for years.)

Of course, you can also line the pan with foil every time you use it, which would definitely help prevent some of the baked-on mess. Our personal preference is to limit the amount of disposable products we use (out of respect for the environment)—but we're not judging! In fact, you will see that we do use foil in a number of recipes—to form packets, keep food warm, and so on. We just try to limit the use to when it has a specific culinary application.

It is important to note that we use cooking spray on the commercial-style pan, but never on our nonstick pans (of any sort). Cooking spray gets baked into the surface and forms a sort of tacky coating—which eventually turns nonstick pans into sticky pans.

## WIRE RACK

You'll need a wire rack—like a cookie cooling rack—that just fits into or is slightly larger than your sheet pan. We sometimes use this to cook in two layers, such as when we cook rice in the bottom of the pan and a steak on the rack.

## SKILLET

All the skillet recipes in the book were developed using a 12-inch pan. We tested them in both nonstick and enamel-coated cast iron (which is nearly nonstick).

### NONSTICK

The best nonstick skillets are made from heavy gauge hard anodized aluminum and have multiple coatings of nonstick so they don't peel. A really good nonstick pan allows you to use less oil and still get beautiful browning. And, of course, you don't have to worry about food getting stuck (yep, that would be the "non" in nonstick) and burning onto the surface—these pans will always be easy to clean. The Anolon nonstick we cook with is dishwasher safe, but we choose to wash it by hand. It is also safe to use with metal utensils . . . but why would we? (We'll talk about utensils below.) In other words, we take care of our nonstick pans more carefully than the manufacturer suggests, and they last really well. It is worth noting that we use our nonstick skillet when developing recipes for magazines and other clients. That means we often cook four to eight dinners a day—which makes us crash-test dummies for cookware.

Before you buy nonstick cookware, be sure it can withstand oven temperatures of at least 425°F. (Our nonstick skillet can go in the oven up to 500°F.) Many recipes in this book call for searing food in the skillet on the stove and finishing it in the oven.

## ENAMEL-COATED CAST IRON

This is cast iron without the maintenance. Coated cast iron holds and conducts heat the way regular cast iron does and is nearly nonstick. To put it another way, we wouldn't try to cook scrambled eggs in enamel-coated cast iron with no oil or butter (as we could in nonstick), but it is easy to clean and requires less oil than a regular pan. When we are going from stovetop to oven, we especially like the way cast iron holds the heat.

When we are making a dish that we want to serve right out of the pan, such as Jambalaya (page 188) or Paella (page 192), we use enamel-coated cast iron, which has a lovely homey look on the table.

Our two top choices are Anolon Vesta pans (which you will see in many photos in this book) and Le Creuset. The Vesta pan is lighter (though be warned—it is still heavy, especially when filled with food!) and about half the price of Le Creuset. Le Creuset is beautiful and will last a lifetime (although we would rather invest in one of their Dutch ovens).

## KNIVES

Every home cook needs three basic knives: a chef's knife (8 to 12 inches), a serrated knife (for cutting bread, tomatoes, and anything else with a resistant exterior and soft interior), and a paring knife. We love our Wüsthofs—but use whatever knives work for you. Just keep them sharp, for safety's sake. A dull knife is much more likely to cause injury.

## MIXING BOWLS

Get a set of inexpensive, nested, wide-mouthed bowls that fit in your dishwasher. Deeper, narrow bowls, shaped more like the ones that come with your stand mixer, make tossing ingredients more challenging. Also, bear in mind that whatever you are tossing or mixing should take up no more than one-third the volume of the bowl to allow you to get nice, even distribution without sending food flying around your kitchen.

## INSTANT-READ MEAT THERMOMETER

Chicken must be cooked to a safe internal temperature to avoid serious foodborne illness. You have two choices: you can cook it to smithereens, or you can have moist, tender, juicy chicken cooked to just the right degree of doneness by cooking to temperature. See page 14 for instructions on how to take a chicken's temperature. (Hint: you can't just feel its forehead.)

## OFFSET TURNERS

These are wide spatulas that are set off from the handle, to make reaching into a pan easier. We like the OXO flexible turners, which are made of silicone and can survive years of dishwashing. They are the perfect size for lifting a piece of chicken out of a skillet; two of them (one at each end) can lift a long fish fillet without breaking it.

## MICROPLANE

The single best way we know to zest citrus.

## TONGS

We can't live without our 9-inch tongs with nylon heads. The coated tips are great on delicate food and nonstick pans, and thanks to the locking feature, they store efficiently in the drawer.

## WOODEN SPOONS

How else would you stir pasta, stews, and vegetables? And what could do a better job of breaking up the crumbles of ground beef? How could you even make sauce without your trusty wooden spoon??? They are perfectly suited to nonstick surfaces and won't cut through delicate food. Wooden spoons have been around forever— for good reason.

## SILICONE SPATULAS

These are better than the old rubber spatulas, though they are shaped the same. When made of silicone, they are more heat resistant and won't melt when used in a hot pan. Get one small enough to fit inside a mustard jar and one standard size.

## BLENDER

A good, ordinary, old-fashioned blender is sometimes better than a big fancy one, and here's why: the big blender is great at pureeing a whole lot of stuff, but doesn't do as good a job blending a small amount of sauce.

## PLASTIC RULER

When a recipe calls for cutting an ingredient into ½-inch dice, the cooking time is predicated on that size. If you cut your squash bigger, for example, it might still be crunchy by the time the beef is cooked through, and if it is too small, it will turn to mush by the time the beef is cooked to the right degree of doneness. Once you measure several times, you will get an eye for it—and your perfectly sized cuts will make all your food taste better! We like a plastic ruler, which is easy to wipe clean.

# POWER MOVES

Did you know you can cook rice in your sheet pan? Or pasta right in the sauce in the skillet? This book is filled with techniques that make it easy to prepare a great, complete meal in just a skillet or sheet pan.

## ADDING FOOD IN STAGES IS KEY

The fact is, you (usually) can't just throw your protein, vegetable, and starch together in a skillet or sheet pan and have your food turn out well. Here's why: if we put broccoli, chicken thighs, and potatoes on a sheet pan and cook it all until the chicken is at a safe internal temperature, that might take about 35 minutes. By then, the broccoli will have turned to gray mush. The potato might be cooked through, but because it was too crowded on the pan, it will have steamed and not browned. It's all edible—but not delicious.

Instead, let's roast the potatoes 5 minutes, then add the chicken and roast for 20 minutes. By then, the potatoes will have formed a beautiful golden crust. Then we'll add the broccoli, and 15 minutes later, just before taking it all out of the oven, we'll sprinkle the crisp-tender broccoli with cheese and let it melt. We've retained the best traits of each component of the meal and not muddled all the flavors together.

The same thing happens for many skillet dishes. If we cooked bacon, shrimp, garlic, arugula, and white beans all together in a skillet, it would be—well, to put it nicely, unappetizing. Now think of cooking that same bacon by itself; take it out of the pan and use some of the drippings to brown the garlic, wilt the arugula, and heat the creamy white beans. Now toss that with crumbled bacon and sear herb-crusted shrimp in the skillet. It's a fantastic meal because you allowed each featured ingredient to really shine—and they don't all taste alike. *You cooked this great meal in just 15 minutes, and all in one pan!* Now that's a hero dinner.

## BROWN IS BEAUTIFUL

Picture the enticing brown crinkly edges of a perfectly cooked pork chop, the golden crust on salmon, the sable sear on the outside of a steak, the bronzed surface of a roasted potato, and the charred leaves on Brussels sprouts. Those appealing images are brought to you courtesy of the Maillard reaction, which makes food more tempting to us humans.

The Maillard reaction, aka browning, is what happens when the proteins and sugars in food are enhanced and transformed by heat. It's why we love crisp chicken skin—and why gray steak is a turn-off.

Many of the recipes in this book put the Maillard reaction to good use. In other words, we make sure that chicken skin crackles, creamy potatoes are encased in a beautiful crust, and so forth. We tell you when it is okay to crowd the pan (because you have already browned, or you want to steam) and when it is not. That, of course, brings us full circle to the point above: *adding food in stages is key.*

## SEASON MEAL COMPONENTS SEPARATELY

The most satisfying meals are often made up of a variety of flavors and textures. Think about how much we love to dunk crusty bread in stew, eat crunchy slaw with a fish sandwich, and dive into creamy potatoes with chewy beef.

The meals in *Hero Dinners* have been developed with our need for variety in mind. It is one reason we so often season components separately—we don't want everything on our dinner plate to taste the same.

Of course, there are exceptions to this, like a skillet full of Rigatoni with Meat Sauce (page 90). But even then, we suggest you serve it with a fresh green salad (and give you the recipe for our indispensable Shallot Vinaigrette, page 91).

## SUPER SIDEKICKS

These are the meal enhancers that make magic happen. With very little work, they add a powerful flavor boost to your meal. And they are interchangeable. Just because we pair a blender sauce with fish doesn't mean you can't also use it on top of chicken. Consider these sidekicks your flavor arsenal: pull one out to make any and every meal you cook that much more delicious.

To make it easy, we list the ingredients and directions separately within each recipe.

### SPICES AND RUBS

We hope you will meet new and interesting herbs and spices when you make these recipes. We also hope some of the combinations will thrill you to the core. When that happens, make a big batch and keep them in an emptied spice jar or small plastic bag in your spice drawer.

- Turmeric Spice Rub (page 34)
- Coriander Herb Crust (page 63)
- Anchovy-Herb Rub (page 78)
- Rosemary Rub (page 132)

### BLENDER SAUCES AND DRESSINGS

There are many simple sauces and dressings on these pages that go beautifully with lots of other meals. You can whip any of these up in about 5 minutes (or less!), and many keep well for several days in the refrigerator.

#### SAUCES AND DRESSINGS
- Caesar Dressing (page 23)
- Ají Verde (page 36)
- Italian Salsa Verde (page 127)
- Arugula-Parsley Pesto (page 135)
- Tzatziki (page 140)
- Lemon-Basil Mayo (page 149)

- Ajvar (page 172)
- Pepita-Spinach Pesto (page 232)
- Peanut Sauce (page 234)

### VINAIGRETTES
- Shallot Vinaigrette (page 91)
- Dijon-Balsamic Vinaigrette (page 110)
- Parsley Vinaigrette (page 137)
- Bacon-Chive Vinaigrette (page 201)
- Sherry Vinaigrette (page 212)

## SIMPLE NO-COOK SIDES

There is no rule that says each component of the meal has to be cooked on the stove or in the oven—or that it has to be cooked at all. There are times a loaf of crusty bread makes the perfect accompaniment and rounds out the meal. Other times, a crisp green salad with a really good vinaigrette is just the thing. Frozen cooked rice, which gets microwaved, or grains that get soaked in hot water but not cooked—these are minimally processed/whole foods that require little effort but get a well-balanced, healthful meal on the table. When one of these no-cook sides completes the meal, it is included with the recipe so you never have to guess. In addition, some of the recipes have no-cook sides you can serve any time, including:

- Quick Pickled Vegetables (page 20)
- Jicama-Radish Salad (page 69)
- Mango-Cabbage Slaw (page 102)
- Olive-Artichoke Salad (page 171)
- Hummus (page 240)
- Pico de Gallo (page 242)

## PANTRY POWER

A carefully curated selection of grains, condiments, herbs and spices, and minimally processed canned goods makes putting together a hero dinner easy, fast, and pleasurable. Bear in mind that the pantry consists of more than the shelves in a cabinet or closet: it is also your freezer and the longer-keeping items in your refrigerator, such as cheese or lemons and limes.

## SALT

We use iodized fine sea salt, which has the pure, clean taste of salt. The flavor of standard table salt has a chemical bite to it in comparison—something you are more likely to notice if you taste them side by side. Table salt and fine sea salt measure the same—that is, you get the same amount of saltiness in every teaspoon. Kosher salt measures a little differently, but that also may be substituted.

## DRIED HERBS AND SPICES

Expanding the herbs and spices you use in your everyday cooking can make a big difference. A chicken thigh roasted with just salt and pepper is good. A chicken thigh roasted with a mixture of cumin, coriander, turmeric, ground ginger, and brown sugar is great. You get all that flavor with just about no work: you simply measure out spices.

The best way to learn to use dried herbs and spices that you are not familiar with is to follow recipes that call for them. You'll get to know not only what they taste like but how much you need to use to impart the right amount of flavor.

- Berbere (see page 49)
- Ground cumin
- Ground cardamom
- Ground coriander
- Ground fennel seed
- Chipotle chile powder

- Ancho chile powder
- Smoked paprika
- Turmeric
- Basil
- Oregano
- Thyme

## VINEGARS

- Balsamic: sweet, with a caramel-like flavor
- Red wine: classic for vinaigrettes
- Sherry: a distinctive flavor unlike any other vinegar; often used in Spanish dishes
- White wine: neutral flavor
- Cider: slight fruitiness, less acidic tasting
- Seasoned rice: lightly sweetened, with gentle acidity

## OILS

- Olive (regular and extra virgin): We generally use regular olive oil as a cooking medium to coat the pan or the food, and extra virgin when we want the oil to add flavor. There are exceptions: we sometimes sweat (or soften) vegetables in extra virgin oil if we want the more robust flavor in the dish, and we use regular olive oil in blender sauces because the whirring motion of the blender causes extra virgin olive oil to take on a bitter flavor.
- Canola: flavorless and healthful
- Sesame: deep, toasty, and nutty flavor

## SWEETENERS

- Sugar: Many dishes benefit from even one teaspoon of sugar. It may not make the dish taste sweet but will help balance the bite of acidic or sour ingredients.
- Jam: an ingredient in many glazes
- Honey: for floral sweetness

## GRAINS, PASTA, AND RICE

- Rice
  - Frozen precooked microwavable rice, white and brown, with no added ingredients
  - Quick-cooking brown rice (we use Uncle Ben's): cooks in both the sheet pan and a skillet
  - Long-grain white rice: cooks in both the sheet pan and a skillet
- Couscous
  - Regular and whole wheat: simply soaks in hot water
  - Israeli (pearl) couscous (aka ptitim): round balls of pasta about the size of small pearls; it is toasted rather than dried, which gives it a nutty flavor and chewy texture (see page 154).
- Bulgur: soaked rather than cooked
- Pasta: a variety of shapes and sizes
- Rice noodles: Many needn't be cooked; they are simply soaked in hot water (read the label before you buy)
- Precooked polenta: comes in a tube; it is sliced into rounds before cooking
- Quick-cooking grits: ready in just 5 minutes

## POTATOES

Potatoes are nature's unprocessed starch and because they are unprocessed, they retain more of their healthful nutrients. Small potatoes, or potatoes cut in small pieces, are a great way to round out a one-pan meal. Besides, who doesn't love roasted potatoes? There are many varieties of potatoes to choose from, each with its unique characteristics. Below are the ones we use in this book.

- Purple: high in antioxidants, nutty with a somewhat grainy texture, hold their shape when cooked

- Yukon Gold: creamy, buttery
- Red: high moisture, hold their shape well
- Fingerling: long and thin (rather than round), thin-skinned and buttery, they may be red, orange, yellow, or white
- Russet/Idaho: fluffy, low moisture, they soak up liquid, can disintegrate in stews (which can help thicken the liquid), and are great for baking and mashing
- Baby (or petite): creamy, smooth, with a concentrated flavor in all colors; fast, even cooking
- Sweet potatoes: nutritional powerhouses with loads of beta-carotene and fiber—and they taste so good!

## CONDIMENTS AND BOTTLED SAUCES

- Harissa: spicy North African paste/sauce
- Bottled salsa verde: the green salsa used in Tex-Mex dishes
- Sriracha: everybody's favorite tangy, garlicky hot sauce
- Louisiana hot sauce: a must for jambalaya and as a flavor boost for vinaigrettes and mayo
- Mustard: Dijon and yellow
- Canola mayonnaise: healthier than classic mayonnaise, but with no compromise of flavor (page 151)
- Green curry paste: fiery, herbaceous, and acidic
- Hoisin: an intensely salty and sweet Chinese sauce made from soybeans, sugar, garlic, five-spice powder, and chilies
- Asian chili-garlic sauce: an intense source of heat often used in stir-fries
- Oyster-flavored sauce: thick and salty, with a strong shellfish flavor

- Fish sauce: adds deep savory flavor; should be used in moderation
- Lower-sodium soy sauce: we prefer to get the soy sauce flavor with less salt (you can always add salt to the dish at the end)
- Tahini: slightly bitter sesame paste that is a must in hummus and great in salad dressings

## FROZEN VEGETABLES

- Corn
- Peas
- Artichokes
- Edamame

## CANNED GOODS

- Tomatoes: diced, petite diced, fire-roasted, paste
- Olives: Kalamata, green pimiento-stuffed
- Capers: nonpareil
- Beans (low-sodium): chickpeas, black beans, red kidney beans, cannellini, lentils; Goya low sodium and organic brands, which are lower in sodium and tend to be firmer (less mealy) and taste more like the bean and less like tin and salt
- Oil-packed anchovy fillets
- Oil-packed sun-dried tomatoes

## NUTS AND SEEDS

- Chestnuts: cooked, shelf stable (no added ingredients)
- Almonds: unblanched (skin on), whole and sliced
- Peanuts: cocktail (oil-roasted and salted)
- Cashews: roasted and salted
- Walnuts: halves and pieces
- Pecans: halves and pieces
- Pistachios: shelled

- Pepitas/pumpkin seeds: raw, shelled
- Sesame seeds

## BROTH

- Unsalted chicken broth: the less sodium there is in broth, the more you taste broth, rather than just salt. You can always add salt to taste at the end of cooking! Our absolute favorite, for its pure Grandma's-chicken-soup flavor, is Kitchen Basics.
- Low-sodium vegetable broth: we like the Pacific brand

## CHEESE

- Crumbled feta
- Cheddar/Dubliner
- Grated Parmesan
- Pecorino
- Asiago

In addition, our freezer always holds:

- Frozen shrimp
- Andouille sausage

And we would consider the refrigerator bare if we didn't have these long-lasting items:

- Cured chorizo
- Lemons, limes, oranges
- Eggs

# 1

# CHICKEN, DUCK, AND TURKEY

## HOW TO MAKE TENDER, JUICY (NEVER DRY!) CHICKEN—EVERY TIME

Many people overcook chicken to be sure it is safe—but then it is like eating cardboard. So how do we ensure chicken is cooked enough to be safe, but not so much that it is dry and flavorless? Very simple: we take its temperature.

While you can often tell a human's temperature by feeling his forehead, that certainly doesn't work with chickens. Contrary to popular belief, you also cannot judge that chicken is cooked to a safe internal temperature by the color of the meat, juiciness, or color of the juices. (Forget the old "until the juices run clear"; it just isn't accurate.)

An instant-read meat thermometer makes temperature-taking easy. For tender, juicy, tasty chicken, cook breasts to 160°F and chicken thighs to 170°F.

When you use an instant-read thermometer, keep in mind the following:

The tip of the wand should be inserted into the center of the thickest part of the largest piece of chicken. (You don't need to check every piece.) The wand should not touch the bone and should always be inserted at least 1 inch into the meat. If your piece of chicken is not 2 inches high—meaning the wand inserted vertically could not end up in the center—insert the thermometer horizontally.

If you insert the thermometer into chicken and it registers *under* 160°F, wash it in hot soapy water before inserting it back into the meat.

# CHICKEN AND EGGPLANT MARGHERITA

ITALIAN SEMOLINA BREAD

6 slices bacon, chopped

1½ pounds boneless, skinless chicken breast halves, cut across into 1-inch-thick slices

¾ teaspoon salt, divided

½ teaspoon ground black pepper, divided

1 medium eggplant (about 1 pound), unpeeled, cut across into ½-inch-thick rounds, and each round quartered

1 tablespoon olive oil

1 medium onion, coarsely chopped (about 1 cup)

6 garlic cloves, minced

1 tablespoon drained nonpareil capers

¼ teaspoon crushed red pepper flakes (or to taste)

1 (14.5-ounce) can diced fire-roasted tomatoes

4 ounces fresh mozzarella, cut into scant ¼-inch-thick slices

¼ cup fresh basil leaves

SKILLET
CHICKEN BREASTS

This is for those nights when you crave the unadulterated pleasure of old-fashioned red-sauce Italian. Slabs of melted mozzarella top chunks of soft, meaty eggplant, bits of still-crisp bacon, and tender chicken—all simmered in smoky tomato sauce. Serve it with Italian semolina bread to round out the meal.

Browning the ingredients in stages may seem like extra work, but it is worth it. The process enhances the distinct flavors and helps build the character of the final dish—and dinner will still be on the table in less than 45 minutes.

MAKES 4 SERVINGS

1. Preheat the oven to 400°F.
2. Cook the bacon in a large ovenproof skillet over medium heat, stirring occasionally, until lightly crisped, 6 to 7 minutes. Transfer to a plate lined with paper towels to drain.
3. Season the chicken with ½ teaspoon of the salt and ¼ teaspoon of the pepper. Increase the heat to medium-high and add the chicken to the skillet; cook, turning once, until it is lightly browned, about 4 minutes. (It will not be cooked through at this point.) Transfer the chicken to a medium bowl.
4. Reduce the heat to medium and add the eggplant to the skillet; cook until it is tender and golden, 5 to 6 minutes. Transfer to the bowl with the chicken.
5. Heat the oil in the skillet; add the onion and cook until it just begins to soften, 1 to 2 minutes. Add the garlic, capers, and red pepper flakes and cook, stirring, for 1 minute. Stir in the tomatoes and cook until the sauce starts to thicken, about 3 minutes. Return the chicken and eggplant (and any juices in the bowl) to the pan; add the remaining ¼ teaspoon salt and ¼ teaspoon pepper and stir well.
6. Bake for 10 minutes. Stir in the bacon and top with the mozzarella; bake until the cheese melts, 1 to 2 minutes. Remove from the oven and top with the basil.

# LEMON CHICKEN WITH ARTICHOKES

ORZO

2 tablespoons olive oil, divided

1 (9-ounce) package frozen artichoke hearts, thawed

1 teaspoon salt, divided

½ teaspoon ground black pepper, divided

4 (6-ounce) boneless, skinless chicken breast halves

2 tablespoons unsalted butter

1 medium onion, cut into ½-inch pieces

3 garlic cloves, minced

1½ cups orzo pasta (about 8 ounces)

¼ cup fresh lemon juice

2½ cups unsalted chicken broth

2 tablespoons chopped fresh parsley

SKILLET
CHICKEN BREASTS

## ARTICHOKES

*We have found that frozen artichokes have a cleaner, more distinct flavor than canned. Look for unseasoned frozen artichokes with no added ingredients.*

David created this dish specifically because I love artichokes so much—but I also love the way the orzo gets a nearly buttery quality as it cooks.

This dinner epitomizes all things good about one-pan cooking. Each element retains its own flavor and texture, and the end result is one of those easy-to-eat dinners we can't wait to sit down to (especially after a long day). And the wait won't be long: from the time you walk into the kitchen to the time dinner is on the table is just over half an hour.

### MAKES 4 SERVINGS

1. Preheat the oven to 400°F.
2. Heat 1 tablespoon of the oil in a large ovenproof skillet over medium-high heat. Add the artichoke hearts, ¼ teaspoon of the salt, and ⅛ teaspoon of the pepper and cook, stirring occasionally, until lightly browned, 3 to 4 minutes. Transfer to a bowl.
3. Season the chicken with ½ teaspoon of the salt and ¼ teaspoon of the pepper. Add the remaining 1 tablespoon oil to the skillet and reduce the heat to medium. Add the chicken to the skillet and cook, turning once, until lightly browned on both sides, about 8 minutes. Transfer to a plate.
4. Melt the butter in the skillet over medium heat and add the onion and garlic; cook, stirring occasionally, until it begins to soften, 1 to 2 minutes. Add the orzo and cook until it is lightly toasted, 2 to 3 minutes. Add the lemon juice and cook, stirring, for 30 seconds. Return the artichoke hearts to the pan and stir in the broth and the remaining ¼ teaspoon salt and ⅛ teaspoon pepper. Bring the mixture to a boil, nestle the chicken breasts on top of the orzo, and transfer to the oven.
5. Bake until an instant-read thermometer inserted horizontally into the center of the chicken registers 160°F and the orzo is cooked through, about 15 minutes. Stir in the parsley just before serving.

# CHICKEN BÁNH MÌ

## QUICK PICKLED VEGETABLES

¼ cup seasoned rice vinegar

¼ cup sugar

¼ teaspoon salt

1 cup preshredded carrots (matchstick size)

1 small daikon radish, peeled and cut into matchsticks (about 1 cup)

½ cup thinly sliced red onion

1 tablespoon fish sauce

2 tablespoons sriracha sauce, divided

¼ teaspoon salt

¼ teaspoon ground black pepper

1½ pounds boneless, skinless chicken breast halves, pounded to an even thickness

½ cup canola mayonnaise

1 tablespoon canola oil

4 (7-to 8-inch) steak or sub rolls, halved horizontally

½ English cucumber, cut diagonally into sixteen ¼-inch-thick slices

⅓ cup fresh mint leaves

⅓ cup fresh cilantro leaves

1 large jalapeño pepper, thinly sliced

## SKILLET
## CHICKEN BREASTS

I was lucky enough to explore Vietnam with my dad, an intrepid traveler then in his mid-eighties. It was there I had the real deal: bánh mì at some of the most (and least!) renowned tiny street shops.

This dish borrows heavily from those I tasted on my memorable trip, but we've left out the pâté to make the sandwiches more accessible, and changed the pork to chicken. (You can certainly also use thinly sliced roasted pork tenderloin.)

Toasting the bread is key: in Vietnam, the first bite into a bánh mì sends shards of crispy crust flying. That's texture #1. Next, just after your teeth sink into the soft bread (texture #2), you hit the crunchy pickled vegetables (#3) that give the sandwich its bright, sharp flavors. Then there's the chewiness of the tender roasted meat (#4) topped with grassy sprigs of cilantro and mint. Finally, when you hit upon that slice of fiery chili, don't expect the creamy mayonnaise to save you—it is kicked up with sriracha. The only thing to do is start all over again. First, the bread . . .

**MAKES 4 SERVINGS**

1. Make the quick pickled vegetables: Combine the vinegar, sugar, and salt in a medium bowl; stir until the sugar dissolves. Add the carrots, daikon, and onion; let it stand at room temperature, giving it a stir now and then, for 30 minutes.

2. Preheat the oven to 350°F.

3. Combine the fish sauce, 1 tablespoon of the sriracha, salt, and pepper in a bowl; add the chicken and toss well. Let it stand at room temperature for 10 minutes.

4. Combine the remaining 1 tablespoon sriracha and the mayonnaise in a small bowl.

5. Heat the oil in a large ovenproof skillet over medium heat. Add the chicken and cook until the underside is golden brown and the chicken readily releases from the pan, 5 to 6 minutes. Turn and

cook until an instant-read thermometer inserted horizontally into the center of the chicken registers 160°F, another 5 to 6 minutes. Transfer the chicken to a cutting board and let rest for 5 minutes.

6. Meanwhile, place the rolls in the oven directly on the oven rack and toast for 5 minutes.

7. Drain the pickled vegetables.

8. Cut the chicken across in ¼- to ½-inch-thick slices. Spread the mayonnaise on the cut surfaces of the rolls and fill each with one-quarter of the chicken, 4 cucumber slices, one-quarter of the pickled vegetables, whole mint and cilantro leaves, and jalapeño slices. Cut each sandwich across in half just before serving.

# DECONSTRUCTED CHICKEN CAESAR SALAD

## CAESAR DRESSING

¼ cup canola mayonnaise

2 oil-packed anchovy fillets, drained, mashed to a paste with a fork

1 tablespoon fresh lemon juice

1 small garlic clove, minced

2 teaspoons Dijon mustard

1 teaspoon Worcestershire sauce

¼ teaspoon ground black pepper

¼ cup olive oil

2 romaine hearts, halved lengthwise

2 tablespoons olive oil, divided

1 pound boneless, skinless chicken breast halves

1 teaspoon Dijon mustard

½ teaspoon chopped fresh thyme

1 demi-baguette (about 12 inches), cut across into 12 slices

½ cup shredded Parmesan cheese

SHEET PAN
CHICKEN BREASTS

This go-to meal, ready in less than 20 minutes, has all the elements of a classic chicken Caesar salad—but instead of tossing them together, we celebrate each on its own.

We believe this is the only Caesar dressing you'll ever need. We stir in a little grated Parmesan and use it as a dip, too.

Roasting romaine hearts intensifies their flavor: you get a slight pleasantly bitter note and a not-so-slight sweetness from the caramelization process. (We love the charred edges!) Small crunchy toasts make a heartier stand-in for croutons, and we cook the chicken breasts, tossed with a touch of mustard and thyme, until they *just* hit 160°F to ensure they are moist and tender.

**MAKES 4 SERVINGS**

1. Position one oven rack 4 to 5 inches below the heat source (leave the other rack in the center of the oven) and preheat the broiler. Coat a sheet pan with cooking spray.
2. Make the Caesar dressing: Combine the mayonnaise, anchovy paste, lemon juice, garlic, mustard, Worcestershire sauce, and pepper in a small bowl. Slowly whisk in the oil.
3. Brush the cut sides of the romaine hearts with 1 tablespoon of the oil. Place them, cut side up, on the sheet pan. Broil the romaine hearts until they are slightly wilted and lightly browned, 1½ to 2 minutes. Transfer to a platter.
4. Preheat the oven to 425°F.
5. Toss the chicken with the remaining 1 tablespoon oil, the mustard, and thyme. Place the breasts and the bread slices on the sheet pan and roast in the center of the oven until an instant-read thermometer inserted horizontally into the center of the chicken registers 160°F and the bread is toasted, 8 to 9 minutes.
6. Transfer the chicken to a cutting board. Let it rest 5 minutes before cutting it across into ¼-inch-thick slices. Place the chicken and toasts on the platter with the romaine; drizzle with the dressing and sprinkle with the Parmesan.

# GREEN CHICKEN ENCHILADAS 2.0

1½ pounds boneless, skinless chicken breast halves

2 tablespoons olive oil

1 medium onion, thinly sliced (about 1 cup)

4 garlic cloves, minced

1 medium red bell pepper, thinly sliced

1 medium green bell pepper, thinly sliced

2 serrano peppers, finely chopped

1½ teaspoons ground cumin

1 teaspoon chili powder

1 (15-ounce) can low-sodium pinto beans, drained and rinsed

1 (16-ounce) jar mild salsa verde

½ teaspoon salt

10 corn tortillas, quartered

½ cup sour cream

1 cup shredded sharp Cheddar cheese

SKILLET
CHICKEN BREASTS

Welcome to the updated, faster, more versatile version of green chicken enchiladas. This update has all the great flavor of the original, but in a new format. Instead of individual rolls, shredded chicken, pinto beans, torn tortillas, and vegetables simmer together in green chile sauce and are finished with a generous amount of shredded Cheddar.

You can cook the chicken 1 to 2 days ahead if you like; or to make the dish even more quickly, use a store-bought rotisserie chicken.

**MAKES 4 SERVINGS**

1. Fill a large ovenproof skillet about three-quarters full with water and bring it to a simmer over medium heat. Add the chicken and cook, turning it over occasionally, until an instant-read thermometer inserted into the thickest part of the chicken registers 160°F. Remove the chicken from the skillet and let it stand until it is cool enough to handle, about 10 minutes. Shred the chicken by pulling it into strands with two forks or with your fingers. You should end up with about 4 cups.

2. Preheat the oven to 425°F.

3. Discard the liquid in the skillet. Add the oil and heat over medium heat. Add the onion, garlic, bell peppers, serranos, cumin, and chili powder and cook, stirring occasionally, until the vegetables are softened, 6 to 7 minutes. Stir in the chicken, pinto beans, salsa verde, and salt and cook, stirring occasionally, for 5 minutes or until heated through. Remove the pan from the heat and stir in the tortillas, sour cream, and ½ cup of the Cheddar.

4. Sprinkle the top with the remaining ½ cup Cheddar and bake until it melts, 4 to 5 minutes. Let it stand at least 5 minutes before serving.

# DUBLINER AND TOMATO-STUFFED CHICKEN BREASTS

POTATO COINS + ZUCCHINI STICKS

3 tablespoons olive oil, divided

2 bone-in skin-on chicken breast halves (about 2½ pounds)

4 ounces Dubliner (or Cheddar) cheese, cut into thin slices

1 plum tomato, cut lengthwise into 4 (¼-inch-thick) slices

4 large fresh parsley leaves

¾ teaspoon salt, divided

¼ teaspoon ground black pepper, divided

2 russet potatoes (about 1 pound), scrubbed and cut across into ¼-inch-thick rounds

2 medium zucchini (about 1 pound)

SHEET PAN
CHICKEN BREASTS

This is the sort of dish that makes its way into the weeknight rotation and stays there for years. It is universally appealing (seriously: chicken + cheese + tomato), and unbelievably simple to put together. Make this chicken once and you will probably never need the recipe again, even though you'll make it over and over.

We use Kerrygold Dubliner cheese, made from the milk of grass-fed cows in Ireland. We love its nutty, complex flavor, but any Cheddar works. (Dubliner, by the way, also comes in a reduced-fat version that knocks our socks off.)

**MAKES 4 SERVINGS**

1. Preheat the oven to 425°F. Brush a sheet pan with 1 tablespoon of the oil.

2. Cut each chicken breast half across into two roughly equal pieces. Working with one piece at a time, loosen the skin but don't completely remove it. Place one-quarter of the cheese directly on the flesh, followed by a tomato slice, and top with a flattened parsley leaf. Slide and stretch the skin to cover. Season the stuffed chicken breast pieces with ¼ teaspoon of the salt and ⅛ teaspoon of the pepper.

3. Combine the potatoes, 1 tablespoon of the oil, and ¼ teaspoon of the salt in a medium bowl. Arrange the potatoes in a single layer on the sheet pan and roast for 10 minutes. Remove the sheet pan from the oven, flip the potatoes, and place the chicken on the pan (it can sit right on top of some of the potatoes). Roast for 15 minutes.

4. Meanwhile, cut the zucchini across in half; cut each half lengthwise into 4 wedges. Toss with the remaining 1 tablespoon oil, ¼ teaspoon salt, and ⅛ teaspoon pepper.

5. After the chicken has roasted 15 minutes, add the zucchini wedges to the pan. Roast until an instant-read thermometer inserted into the center of the largest piece of chicken registers 160°F and the vegetables are cooked through, about 15 minutes longer.

## TO HALVE AND HALVE NOT

When you buy bone-in chicken breasts, each piece is actually a chicken breast *half*. Those halves have gotten larger over the years—each used to be about the right size for a single serving, but they are now often big enough to serve two. For most dishes, it is best to cut them across into two serving pieces before cooking.

The breast halves are often sold with "rib meat" attached. Really, it's mostly the rib *bones*, and we cut those off and put them in a bag in the freezer for chicken soup.

To cut the breasts in half, first make a clean cut across the meat until your knife comes in contact with the bone. To cut through the bone, put the weight of your blade (the heaviest part closest to the handle) on the bone and rock it back and forth.

# MISO CHICKEN

2 bone-in, skin-on chicken breast halves (about 2½ pounds)

½ teaspoon salt

¼ teaspoon ground black pepper

1 tablespoon canola oil

3 garlic cloves, minced

1 tablespoon minced fresh ginger

2 cups unsalted chicken broth

3 tablespoons white miso paste

2 tablespoons lower-sodium soy sauce

2 carrots, peeled and cut across into ½-inch pieces (about 1 cup)

1 medium white turnip (about 5 ounces), peeled and cut into ½-inch pieces

6 radishes, quartered

¾ cup Israeli (pearl) couscous

3 scallions, cut into ½-inch pieces (about ½ cup)

SKILLET
CHICKEN BREASTS

When David first created a version of this for a client, I fell madly in love with its soothing and subtle salty-sweet broth. It is like an elegant, Asian-influenced version of poule au pot. The gently simmered radishes and turnip add just a hint of bitter bite and crunch, while the generous amount of fresh ginger gives the dish a bright, piquant note.

**MAKES 4 SERVINGS**

1. Preheat the oven to 375°F.
2. Cut the chicken breasts across in half (see page 27) and season them with the salt and pepper. Heat the oil in a large skillet over medium heat. Add the chicken and cook, turning once, until nicely browned, about 8 minutes; transfer to a plate. (They are not yet cooked through.)
3. Add the garlic and ginger to the ovenproof skillet and cook, stirring, until fragrant, about 1 minute. Add the broth, miso paste, and soy sauce, stirring until the miso dissolves. Add the carrots, turnip, and radishes. Cover, bring to a simmer, and cook until the vegetables are slightly tender, about 10 minutes.
4. Stir in the couscous, cover, and cook for 5 minutes. Top with the chicken, cover, and bake until an instant-read thermometer inserted into the center of the largest piece of chicken registers 160°F, 18 to 20 minutes.
5. Sprinkle with the scallions just before serving.

## THE MANY COLORS OF MISO

Miso, the salty paste made from fermented soybeans, is a protein-rich, probiotic ingredient with innumerable health benefits and intense savory flavor. There are many varieties, but the most common are categorized as either white or red miso.

- **WHITE MISO:** Made with rice as well as fermented soybeans, it is slightly sweet and nutty. It is great for salad dressings and sauces, broths when you want light, slightly sweet flavor, and thin glazes for fish and vegetables.

- **RED MISO:** Fermented for much longer than white miso, red miso has a stronger, meatier flavor. We use it with braised meats and to make miso soup.

Miso should be kept in a closed container in the refrigerator, where it can stay indefinitely. Don't worry if the color darkens a little over time, but as with anything, if you notice an off odor or flavor, toss it.

# DIJON-ROASTED CHICKEN AND APPLES

2 bone-in, skin-on chicken breast halves (about 2½ pounds)

2 tablespoons Dijon mustard

3 tablespoons olive oil, divided

¾ teaspoon salt, divided

¼ teaspoon plus ⅛ teaspoon ground black pepper, divided

2 (12-ounce) sweet potatoes, peeled, each cut lengthwise into 8 wedges

2 medium red onions, cut through the root end into 8 wedges each

2 medium Granny Smith apples, peeled and cored, each cut into 8 wedges

SHEET PAN
CHICKEN BREASTS

We first made this dish (without the sweet potatoes) when the kids were little and we'd been overly enthusiastic on our apple-picking adventure. Over the years, it became a ritual: we'd come home from the yearly trip to the orchard and this would be dinner. In recent years, once we'd embraced the pleasure of having only one pan to clean after dinner, we added the sweet potato wedges. This is a really nutritious, satisfying, and complete autumn meal.

We generally like to use tart Granny Smith or Golden Delicious apples for cooking; both keep their texture well. But truly, most any apple will do: we've used Fuji and Gala as well. The one apple we won't use is Macouns—their season is short and we savor those for eating out of hand.

**MAKES 4 SERVINGS**

1. Preheat the oven to 400°F. Coat a sheet pan with cooking spray.
2. Cut the chicken breasts across in half (see page 27). Combine the mustard, 1 tablespoon of the oil, ½ teaspoon of the salt, and ¼ teaspoon of the pepper in a bowl; add the chicken and toss well.
3. Combine the sweet potatoes, onions, and 1 tablespoon of the oil in a bowl. Toss with the remaining ¼ teaspoon salt and ⅛ teaspoon pepper.
4. Arrange the sweet potatoes and onions in a single layer on the sheet pan. Roast the vegetables for 10 minutes.
5. Meanwhile, toss the apples with the remaining 1 tablespoon oil.
6. Push the sweet potatoes and onions to the sides of the pan and arrange the apple wedges in the center. Place the chicken on top of the apples and roast until the chicken is lightly browned and an instant-read thermometer inserted into the center of the largest piece registers 160°F, 33 to 35 minutes.

# CHICKEN WITH EGGPLANT, OLIVES, AND APRICOTS

2 bone-in, skin-on chicken breast halves (about 2½ pounds)

4 tablespoons extra virgin olive oil, divided

Grated zest and juice of 1 lemon

2 garlic cloves, minced

1 teaspoon ground cumin

1 teaspoon salt, divided

½ teaspoon ground black pepper, divided

1 teaspoon dried basil

1 teaspoon ground fennel

2 tablespoons tomato paste

1 large eggplant (about 1½ pounds), unpeeled and cut into 1½-inch pieces

1 medium onion, coarsely chopped (about 1 cup)

2 bell peppers, assorted colors, cut into 1½-inch pieces

½ cup dried apricots, halved

½ cup pitted Kalamata olives, halved lengthwise

1 cup unsalted chicken broth

SHEET PAN
CHICKEN BREASTS

This is a dish with a big personality: the sweet and slightly tart flavor of apricots is the perfect foil for sharp, salty bits of olive; and the meaty texture of eggplant and chicken gives way to the crisp-tender peppers.

Luckily, the riot of flavors and textures requires very little effort from the cook. In fact, after chopping the vegetables, it's a matter of combining ingredients in a bowl and laying them out on the sheet pan. We like to serve this with warmed pitas (the pocketless kind) or Orange Couscous (page 84).

**MAKES 4 SERVINGS**

1.  Cut the chicken breasts across in half (see page 27). Combine the chicken, 1 tablespoon of the oil, the lemon zest, lemon juice, garlic, cumin, ½ teaspoon of the salt, and ¼ teaspoon of the pepper in a medium bowl. Let it stand at room temperature for 30 minutes.
2.  Preheat the oven to 425°F. Coat a sheet pan with cooking spray.
3.  Combine the remaining 3 tablespoons oil, ½ teaspoon salt, ¼ teaspoon black pepper, basil, fennel, and tomato paste in a large bowl. Add the eggplant, onion, and bell peppers; toss well and transfer to the sheet pan.
4.  Roast the vegetables for 15 minutes. Stir in the apricots, olives, and broth. Place the chicken on top of the vegetables and roast until an instant-read thermometer inserted into the center of the largest piece registers 160°F, 36 to 38 minutes.

## SEX, GENDER, AND BITTERNESS: A TALE OF EGGPLANT MALARKEY

Pity the poor eggplant, whose sexual identity is so often misunderstood.

And why, you might wonder, would the gender of an eggplant matter? It is often said that female eggplants have more seeds, and it's the seeds that can make eggplant bitter. The story goes that you determine the gender of an eggplant by examining its bottom (!) to determine the shape of the blossom mark—the beige mark is either round (male) or elongated (female). But the truth is that eggplants are hermaphrodites. Both male and female parts exist in every perfect flower.

When you want to choose an eggplant, sex is clearly not the way to go. Instead, choose an eggplant that is:

- Resilient to the touch. When you press it, the flesh should bounce back.

- Heavy for its size. The more flesh there is, the fewer the seeds.

# SPICE-RUBBED CHICKEN THIGHS

## TURMERIC SPICE RUB

1 teaspoon light brown sugar

1½ teaspoons ground cumin

1 teaspoon garlic powder

½ teaspoon ground turmeric

½ teaspoon ground coriander

¼ teaspoon ground ginger

½ teaspoon salt

¼ teaspoon ground black pepper

2½ pounds bone-in, skin-on chicken thighs (4 to 6 thighs)

1 pound Yukon Gold potatoes, cut into 1½-inch chunks

2 tablespoons extra virgin olive oil, divided

1 teaspoon chopped fresh thyme

½ teaspoon salt, divided

¼ teaspoon ground black pepper

6 cups broccoli florets (about 1¼ pounds)

½ cup shredded Parmesan cheese

SHEET PAN
CHICKEN THIGHS

Turmeric adds beautiful golden color and appealing subtle bitterness to this savory and aromatic rub. We like the balance of flavors so much—from ginger's piquant punch to cumin's earthy depth and the sweet, molassesy note of brown sugar—that we make a big batch and keep it in an emptied spice jar in our cabinet. (You can also keep it in a zip-top plastic bag.) The rub keeps well for several months.

**MAKES 4 SERVINGS**

1. Preheat the oven to 425°F. Coat a sheet pan with cooking spray.
2. Make the spice rub: Combine the brown sugar, cumin, garlic powder, turmeric, coriander, ginger, salt, and pepper in a small bowl. Pat the mixture evenly all over the chicken to coat.
3. Combine the potatoes with 1 tablespoon of the oil in a bowl. Toss with the thyme, ¼ teaspoon of the salt, and the pepper. Arrange in a single layer on the sheet pan and roast for 5 minutes.
4. Remove the pan from the oven, push the potatoes to one side, and add the chicken thighs, skin side up. Roast for 20 minutes.
5. Meanwhile, toss the broccoli florets with the remaining 1 tablespoon oil and ¼ teaspoon salt.
6. Remove the sheet pan from the oven, gently toss the potatoes and again move them over to make room for the broccoli. (The broccoli does not need to be in a single layer.)
7. Roast until the potatoes and broccoli are tender and an instant-read thermometer inserted into the center of the largest piece of chicken registers 170°F, 15 to 17 minutes. Sprinkle the Parmesan over the broccoli and return the pan to the oven until the cheese is melted, about 2 minutes.

## TURMERIC MAGIC

Several years ago, turmeric was "discovered" for its many health properties. In fact, studies show that turmeric extract can help reduce cholesterol and possibly reduce arthritis pain. As much as we would all like to believe in turmeric magic, the truth is that you would need to consume it in concentrated (or extract) form at least a couple of times a day.

On the other hand, cooking with turmeric and many other spices *is* good for you. Not only might there be a synergistic health effect, your food will taste much better! So maybe turmeric is magical after all. . . .

# PERUVIAN CHICKEN WITH AJÍ VERDE

2 tablespoons lower-sodium soy sauce

2 teaspoons sugar

1 teaspoon garlic powder

½ teaspoon chipotle chile powder

½ teaspoon dried thyme

1 teaspoon salt, divided

2½ pounds bone-in, skin-on chicken thighs (4 to 6 thighs)

12 ounces baby purple potatoes, halved lengthwise

12 ounces Brussels sprouts, trimmed and halved lengthwise

2 tablespoons olive oil, divided

½ cup unsalted chicken broth

### AJÍ VERDE

½ cup fresh cilantro leaves

1 jalapeño pepper, seeded

1 small garlic clove

¼ cup sour cream

¼ cup canola mayonnaise

1 tablespoon olive oil

1 teaspoon white wine vinegar

¼ teaspoon salt

SKILLET
CHICKEN THIGHS

When David came back from a business trip to Peru (training chefs there for the United States Poultry and Egg Export Council), he raved about the food. Ají verde, the ubiquitous green sauce he had eaten so often at Peruvian restaurants in the States, had a brighter, more vivid flavor in its homeland.

The savory rub (with just a hint of sugar) on the chicken is also based on the flavors David experienced in Peru.

The ají verde keeps well for several days in the refrigerator. It makes a great dip and pairs as well with fish as it does with poultry.

**MAKES 4 SERVINGS**

1. Preheat the oven to 425°F.
2. Combine the soy sauce, sugar, garlic powder, chipotle powder, thyme, and ½ teaspoon of the salt in a small bowl to form a paste. Rub the mixture all over the chicken to coat.
3. Combine the potatoes, Brussels sprouts, and 1 tablespoon of the oil in a large bowl. Toss with the remaining ½ teaspoon salt.
4. Heat the remaining 1 tablespoon oil in a large ovenproof skillet over medium heat. Add the chicken, skin side down, and cook until well browned, about 4 minutes. Remove the chicken from the skillet and add the potatoes and Brussels sprouts. Place the chicken, skin side up, on top of the vegetables and pour in the broth; cook for 2 minutes. Transfer to the oven and roast until the vegetables are tender and an instant-read thermometer inserted into the center of the largest piece of chicken registers 170°F, 23 to 25 minutes.
5. While the chicken roasts, make the ají verde: Puree the cilantro, jalapeño, garlic, sour cream, mayonnaise, olive oil, vinegar, and salt in a blender.

## THE COLOR PURPLE

Purple potatoes are a highly concentrated source of antioxidants called anthocyanins, which help prevent cancer and reduce the risk of heart disease and Parkinson's. In one small study, participants who ate 6 to 8 golf ball–size purple potatoes a day lowered their blood pressure by the same amount that they would have eating oatmeal. Researchers equate the antioxidant benefit of purple potatoes to that of kale. You don't have to twist our arms!

# ANCHO CHICKEN POT PIE WITH CORNMEAL DROP BISCUIT TOPPING

1½ pounds boneless, skinless chicken thighs, trimmed and cut into 1-inch pieces

¾ teaspoon salt, divided

¼ teaspoon ground black pepper

2 tablespoons canola oil, divided

1 medium onion, cut into ½-inch pieces (about 1 cup)

1 small green bell pepper, cut into ½-inch pieces (about ¾ cup)

1 small red bell pepper, cut into ½-inch pieces (about ¾ cup)

4 garlic cloves, minced

2 teaspoons chili powder

1 teaspoon ancho chile powder

1 teaspoon ground cumin

1 (14.5-ounce) can diced tomatoes

⅔ cup unsalted chicken broth

### CORNMEAL BISCUITS

1¼ cups all-purpose flour

½ cup yellow cornmeal (fine to medium grind)

1 teaspoon baking powder

½ teaspoon salt

4 tablespoons (½ stick) cold unsalted butter, cut into small pieces

¾ cup milk

SKILLET

CHICKEN THIGHS

Ancho chile powder gives this dish an earthy, toasted, almost sweet flavor and just a touch of heat. Made entirely from dried and roasted poblano peppers, ancho powder is very different from "chili powder." Regular chili powder—a ubiquitous ingredient in Tex-Mex dishes—is actually a *blend* of spices, including chiles but also paprika, cumin, garlic and onion powders, sugar, salt, and sometimes wheat flour.

We call this dish a pot pie because it is topped with biscuits, but you could also think of it as a fragrant and hearty chili. In fact, you can make the filling on its own, freeze it, and later top it with these flaky, nutty cornmeal biscuits. The biscuits can be made on their own as well: follow the recipe below and bake them on a sheet pan coated with cooking spray at 400°F until they're golden, 14 to 16 minutes.

**MAKES 4 SERVINGS**

1. Preheat the oven to 400°F.

2. Season the chicken with ½ teaspoon of the salt and the pepper. Heat 1 tablespoon of the oil in a large skillet over medium-high heat. Add half of the chicken to the skillet and cook until lightly browned, turning occasionally, 3 to 4 minutes. Transfer to a plate, add the remaining chicken to the skillet, and repeat.

3. Reduce the heat to medium and heat the remaining 1 tablespoon oil in the skillet. Add the onion and cook, stirring occasionally, until slightly softened, 3 to 4 minutes. Stir in the bell peppers, garlic, and remaining ¼ teaspoon salt and cook until the vegetables begin to soften, 3 to 4 minutes. Add the chili powder, ancho powder, and cumin and cook, stirring, until fragrant, about 30 seconds. Add the diced tomatoes and broth, cover, reduce the heat to medium-low, and simmer for 4 minutes. Stir in the reserved chicken and any juices that have accumulated on the plate. Remove from the heat.

4. Make the biscuits: Combine the flour, cornmeal, baking powder, and salt in a bowl. Use a pastry blender or two knives to cut the butter into the flour mixture until it resembles coarse crumbs. Add

**NEAT TRICK**

*Coat the ¼-cup measure you use to ladle the biscuit batter onto the pot pie with cooking spray. The batter will slide right out of the cup. (This works great when making pancakes, too.)*

the milk and stir until the mixture is just moistened, taking care not to overwork the batter. Drop 8 dollops (a scant ¼ cup each) of batter over the chicken mixture.

5. Transfer the skillet to the oven and bake until the biscuits are golden brown and the filling is bubbling around the edges, about 20 minutes. Let stand 5 minutes before serving.

# FARMERS' MARKET CHICKEN

BROWN RICE + CHERRY TOMATOES + CORN

4 tablespoons extra virgin olive oil, divided

2 tablespoons chopped fresh cilantro

2 tablespoons chopped fresh parsley

1 teaspoon grated lime zest

1 teaspoon salt, divided

½ teaspoon ground black pepper, divided

2 garlic cloves

2½ pounds bone-in, skin-on chicken thighs (4 to 6 thighs)

2 pints cherry tomatoes, assorted colors

1 small onion, cut into ½-inch pieces (about ½ cup)

1½ cups fresh (or frozen) corn kernels

1 cup quick-cooking brown rice

1 cup unsalted chicken broth

SHEET PAN
CHICKEN THIGHS

Whether you make this after visiting a farmers' market or your local grocery store, the idea is the same: the meal is about fresh herbs and vegetables.

You start by cooking the rice on the sheet pan with the corn and tomatoes. As the vegetables cook and soften, they ooze flavor into the rice. Next, chicken thighs tossed with fresh herbs and a squeeze of lime are placed on top of the partially cooked rice and everything roasts together. The happy result is a healthful meal of nutty brown rice speckled with sweet corn, intensely flavored roasted cherry tomatoes, and crisp-skinned herb-crusted chicken.

A note for the cook: We decided long ago that as cooks, we get early access to goodies such as the crusty little browned bits of rice along the edges of the pan. You can certainly be better sharers than us and stir them right into the rice before you serve it.

MAKES 4 SERVINGS

1. Preheat the oven to 425°F. Coat a sheet pan with cooking spray.
2. Combine 2 tablespoons of the oil, the cilantro, parsley, lime zest, ½ teaspoon of the salt, and ¼ teaspoon of the pepper in a large bowl. Grate the garlic into the bowl. Stir, add the chicken, and toss well.
3. Combine the remaining 2 tablespoons oil, the tomatoes, onion, and corn in a bowl. Toss with ¼ teaspoon of the salt and the remaining ¼ teaspoon pepper.
4. Spread the rice on the sheet pan. Combine the broth, 1 cup water, and the remaining ¼ teaspoon salt and pour over the rice. Spoon the tomato/corn mixture over the rice. Roast for 15 minutes.
5. Remove the sheet pan from the oven and top with the chicken thighs. Roast until an instant-read thermometer inserted into the center of the largest piece registers 170°F, the rice is cooked through, and the tomatoes are tender, 30 to 32 minutes.

## MORE THAN ONE WAY TO SLICE (OR MINCE) THAT GARLIC

Believe it or not, there is a difference in flavor when you mince garlic with a knife, use a garlic press, or grate it.

Finely minced garlic cooks up sweet, but the little bits can scorch if they're on the surface of food in the oven. When garlic goes through a press, more of the oils are released, and it tends to be sharp and pungent. Grating garlic is the middle ground: you don't get as many of the harsh oils, but you do get a superfine texture. We typically grate garlic when it is going on the outside of a bird or roast in the oven, or when the garlic won't cook long but we don't want to end up with vampire-slaying breath.

# CHICKEN, SHIITAKE, AND POTATO FRICASSEE

3 tablespoons olive oil, divided

12 ounces shiitake mushrooms, stems discarded and caps cut into ½-inch-wide slices

¾ teaspoon salt, divided

12 ounces red and/or white baby potatoes, quartered lengthwise

1 cup frozen pearl onions, thawed

5 garlic cloves, sliced

1 teaspoon chopped fresh thyme

1 tablespoon all-purpose flour

¼ teaspoon ground black pepper

2½ pounds bone-in, skin-on chicken thighs (4 to 6 thighs)

1½ cups unsalted chicken broth

1 cup frozen peas, thawed

SKILLET
CHICKEN THIGHS

The key to a good skillet dinner is often respecting—and playing up—the individual characteristics of the ingredients. In this skillet, thick slices of shiitake mushrooms, which enhance the meatiness of chicken thighs, are browned first to develop and intensify their savory umami flavor. Rather than let the potatoes just simmer in the sauce, we brown those first, too. Pearl onions add a sweet note; green peas are also sweet and lend grassy crunch. At the center of it all are the chicken thighs, which are lightly dusted with flour to ensure the skin browns and to help thicken the lovely broth.

**MAKES 4 SERVINGS**

1. Heat 2 tablespoons of the oil in a large nonstick skillet over medium-high heat. Add the shiitakes and ¼ teaspoon of the salt and cook, stirring occasionally, until they begin to soften, about 4 minutes. Add the potatoes and cook until they are lightly browned, about 5 minutes. Stir in the pearl onions, garlic, and thyme and cook until the onions start to brown, about 4 minutes. Transfer to a bowl.

2. Combine the flour, pepper, and remaining ½ teaspoon salt in a large bowl. Add the chicken and toss to coat.

3. Heat the remaining 1 tablespoon oil in the skillet over medium-high heat. Add the chicken, skin side down, and cook, turning once, until well browned, about 8 minutes. Transfer the chicken to a plate and pour off all but 1 tablespoon of the fat. Return the chicken to the skillet skin side up.

4. Add the reserved mushroom mixture to the chicken and cook for 1 minute. Pour in the broth and bring to a boil. Reduce the heat to medium-low, cover, and simmer for 15 minutes. Uncover the skillet, increase the heat to medium, and continue simmering until an instant-read thermometer inserted into the center of the largest piece registers 170°F and the liquid is slightly thickened, about 10 minutes. Stir in the peas and cook another 3 minutes.

# CHICKEN AND KOHLRABI

2 tablespoons fresh lemon juice

2 tablespoons extra virgin olive oil

2 garlic cloves, minced

1 teaspoon dried basil

2½ pounds bone-in, skin-on chicken thighs (4 to 6 thighs)

1 teaspoon salt, divided

½ teaspoon ground black pepper, divided

1 tablespoon olive oil

2 kohlrabi (about 1 pound), peeled and cut into ¼-inch-thick half-moons

1 large red bell pepper, cut into 2 x ½-inch-wide strips

1 medium red onion, cut into ½-inch pieces (about 1 cup)

⅓ cup golden raisins

2 cups unsalted chicken broth

1 cup long-grain white rice

3 tablespoons coarsely chopped fresh parsley

**SKILLET**
CHICKEN THIGHS

This dish was one of those happy accidents that happen at the end of a long day when you open the fridge and say, "What can we make for dinner?" We gathered up some of this and a little of that, and a meal was born—one we're now crazy about. It's a comfortable homey dinner that we've made a slew of times and even shared with friends. The combination of crunchy, mild kohlrabi, the occasional sweet hit of golden raisins, the slightly brothy rice, and the tender chicken makes it accessible for the fussier eater but interesting enough for a more adventurous palate.

As a bonus, it makes great leftovers that reheat well.

**MAKES 4 SERVINGS**

1. Combine the lemon juice, extra virgin olive oil, garlic, and basil in a medium bowl; add the chicken and toss well. Let it stand at room temperature for 30 minutes or refrigerate for 2 hours.
2. Preheat the oven to 375°F.
3. Season the chicken with ½ teaspoon of the salt and ¼ teaspoon of the pepper. Heat the olive oil in a large ovenproof skillet over medium heat. Add the chicken and cook, turning once, until browned, about 8 minutes; transfer to a plate.
4. Pour off all but 1 tablespoon of the fat from the skillet. Add the kohlrabi, bell pepper, onion, and raisins and cook, stirring occasionally, until they start to soften, about 2 minutes. Stir in the broth, rice, and the remaining ½ teaspoon salt and ¼ teaspoon pepper. Bring to a simmer and set the chicken on top of the rice and vegetables. Cover, transfer to the oven, and bake for 25 minutes. Uncover the skillet and bake until an instant-read thermometer inserted into the center of the largest piece of chicken registers 170°F and the rice is cooked through, about another 5 minutes. Stir in the parsley before serving.

# KOHLRABI

Kohlrabi is the underdog of the vegetable world. While it grows easily, people don't seem to know what to do with it, which is a shame. This fall and winter vegetable looks and cooks up like a turnip and tastes a little like a cross between broccoli and daikon radish.

- **SHOP:** Look for heavy bulbs with taut skin and leaves that are bright and fresh, not wilted. The skin may be either green or purple, but it gets peeled off and discarded.

- **STORE:** Cut off the leaves and store them in a plastic bag; they should last about 3 days. (Cook them as you would any hardy greens: we like them sautéed with olive oil and garlic and finished with a squeeze of lemon.) The bulbs can go directly in the crisper drawer in your refrigerator, where they will last for weeks.

- **COOK:** You can eat kohlrabi raw: we like its radish-like bite with dips or as thin slices in a salad. Cook it as you would any root vegetable: it can be roasted or sautéed with a little butter and salt.

- **NUTRITION:** 1 cup of raw kohlrabi has 36 calories and 5 grams of fiber and is high in vitamin C and potassium.

# BERBERE CHICKEN STEW

1½ pounds boneless, skinless chicken thighs, cut into 1½-inch pieces

2 tablespoons berbere, divided

2 tablespoons olive oil, divided

1 medium onion, chopped (about 1 cup)

1 medium red bell pepper, cut into ¾-inch pieces (about 1 cup)

1 tablespoon minced fresh ginger

1 (28-ounce) can diced fire-roasted tomatoes

1 large sweet potato (12 ounces), peeled and cut into ¾-inch pieces

½ teaspoon salt

½ cup cocktail peanuts

SKILLET
CHICKEN THIGHS

Berbere, the wildly flavorful Ethiopian spice blend, is especially good paired with dark-meat chicken or beef stew meat and sweet potato. The berbere and sweet potato have an almost symbiotic relationship: the spice makes the potato taste even sweeter and creamier, and the potato helps balance the heat of the chiles. Be warned, though—the sweet potato doesn't make the dish any less fiery.

This stew, while very simple to make, is not for the faint of heart—it is for the heat-loving, big-flavor food adventurist. We like to make this for certain (like-minded) friends, set the pan in the center of the table with a loaf of crusty sourdough bread and a bottle of really lusty red wine, and let everyone help themselves.

**MAKES 4 SERVINGS**

1. Combine the chicken and 1 tablespoon of the berbere in a large bowl and toss well.

2. Heat 1 tablespoon of the oil in a large skillet over medium-high heat. Add the chicken and cook, stirring occasionally, until lightly browned, 4 to 5 minutes. Transfer to a bowl.

3. Reduce the heat to medium and add the remaining 1 tablespoon oil to the skillet. Add the onion, bell pepper, and ginger and cook, stirring occasionally, until the vegetables are slightly softened, 3 to 4 minutes. Stir in the tomatoes, 1 cup water, the sweet potato, salt, and remaining 1 tablespoon berbere. Bring to a simmer and cook, stirring occasionally, until the liquid starts to thicken, about 10 minutes. Stir in the chicken and any juices that have accumulated in the bowl; reduce the heat to medium-low, cover, and simmer, stirring occasionally, for 15 minutes. Uncover the skillet and continue simmering until the sauce has thickened slightly and the vegetables are tender, 7 to 8 minutes.

4. Remove the pan from the heat and stir in the peanuts.

### BERBERE

*Berbere is a spice blend made from ground fiery chiles, fenugreek, and aromatic spices (including cardamom, coriander, clove, cumin, and ground nutmeg). It is now produced by the major spice bottlers, including McCormick and our favorite (available at Whole Foods), Frontier Spice, which means it is available in many grocery stores.*

# DRUMSTICKS OSSO BUCO

2 tablespoons all-purpose flour

1 teaspoon salt, divided

½ teaspoon ground black pepper, divided

8 chicken drumsticks (about 2½ pounds)

2 tablespoons olive oil, divided

1 medium onion, cut into ¼-inch pieces (about 1 cup)

2 celery stalks, cut into ¼-inch pieces (about 1 cup)

2 carrots, peeled and cut into ¼-inch pieces (about 1 cup)

5 garlic cloves, minced

1 teaspoon dried basil

1 teaspoon dried oregano

⅔ cup red wine

1 cup unsalted chicken broth

1 (14.5-ounce) can petite diced tomatoes

2 (10-ounce) bags frozen cooked white rice

SKILLET
DRUMSTICKS

While traditional osso buco is made with veal shanks, we've used the same process and flavors with chicken drumsticks. We brown the drumsticks, then simmer them in a well-seasoned mixture of wine, vegetables, and tomatoes. The result is falling-off-the-bone tender, succulent meat in a heady, rich broth.

Here we've served it over rice, but crusty bread makes an equally good accompaniment.

**MAKES 4 SERVINGS**

1. Combine the flour, ¾ teaspoon of the salt, and ¼ teaspoon of the pepper in a large bowl. Add the drumsticks and toss until the chicken is evenly coated.

2. Heat 1 tablespoon of the oil in a large skillet over medium-high heat. Add the chicken and cook, turning occasionally, until browned on all sides, about 8 minutes. Transfer to a plate.

3. Reduce the heat to medium and add the remaining 1 tablespoon oil to the skillet. Add the onion, celery, carrots, garlic, basil, oregano, and the remaining ¼ teaspoon salt and ¼ teaspoon pepper and cook, stirring occasionally, until the vegetables are softened, 6 to 7 minutes. Add the wine, bring to a boil, and cook for 2 minutes. Stir in the broth and tomatoes and cook until slightly thickened, 10 to 12 minutes. Return the chicken to the skillet, reduce the heat to medium-low, and cover. Simmer gently, turning the chicken occasionally, until an instant-read thermometer inserted parallel to the bone into the widest part of the drumstick registers 170°F, 16 to 18 minutes.

4. Microwave the rice according to package directions. Serve the chicken and plenty of the sauce over a bed of the rice.

# CHARDONNAY CHICKEN

GREEN SALAD WITH SHALLOT VINAIGRETTE + CRUSTY FRENCH BREAD

1 (4-pound) chicken, cut into 8 pieces (see page 55)

1 teaspoon salt, divided

½ teaspoon ground black pepper, divided

2 tablespoons olive oil

6 slices bacon, chopped

1 cup frozen pearl onions, thawed

8 ounces white mushrooms, thinly sliced

2 carrots, peeled, halved lengthwise, and cut across into 1-inch half-moons (about 1 cup)

2 celery stalks, cut into 1-inch chunks (about 1 cup)

4 garlic cloves, minced

2 teaspoons chopped fresh thyme

1 cup Chardonnay or other dry white wine

1 cup unsalted chicken broth

3 tablespoons all-purpose flour

SKILLET
CUT-UP CHICKEN

Years ago, when David worked for a very high-end caterer (they did parties for Bette Midler, Robert Rauschenberg, and Elie Wiesel, among others), he prepared a fancier version of this Chardonnay chicken. We think this simplified version is every bit as good.

The dish is a riff on classic coq au vin—but made with white wine rather than red, which makes the whole dish feel lighter. We like to serve this with a crisp green salad with Shallot Vinaigrette (page 91) and a crusty French bread for dunking into the sauce.

**MAKES 4 SERVINGS**

1. Preheat the oven to 350°F.
2. Season the chicken pieces with ½ teaspoon of the salt and ¼ teaspoon of the pepper. Heat the oil in a large skillet over medium heat. Add the chicken and cook, turning once, until browned, about 8 minutes. Transfer to a plate.
3. Add the bacon to the ovenproof skillet and cook, stirring occasionally, until lightly crisped, 6 to 7 minutes. Use a spoon to hold the bacon back in the pan as you pour off all but about 2 tablespoons of the fat.
4. Add the pearl onions, mushrooms, carrots, celery, garlic, thyme, and the remaining ½ teaspoon salt and ¼ teaspoon pepper to the pan. Cook, stirring occasionally, until the vegetables are slightly softened, 5 to 6 minutes. Pour in the wine, bring to a boil, and cook, stirring to scrape up any browned bits from the bottom of the skillet, until slightly reduced, about 4 minutes.
5. While the wine boils, whisk the broth and flour until smooth.
6. Add the broth mixture to the skillet and cook, stirring, until it is slightly thickened, about 2 minutes.
7. Set the chicken on top of the vegetables, cover the skillet, and transfer to the oven. Bake until the vegetables are tender and an instant-read thermometer inserted into the center of the largest piece of the breast registers 160°F, 31 to 33 minutes.

# BUTTERMILK OVEN-FRIED CHICKEN

1 (4-pound) chicken, cut into 8 pieces (see opposite) and skin removed

2 cups low-fat buttermilk

12 ounces fresh okra

1 tablespoon olive oil

1 teaspoon salt, divided

2 teaspoons garlic powder

1 teaspoon smoked paprika

1 teaspoon ancho chile powder

¼ teaspoon cayenne pepper

1½ cups panko breadcrumbs

4 ears corn

2 tablespoons unsalted butter, softened

SHEET PAN
CUT-UP CHICKEN

Fried chicken is wonderful, but it makes an incredible mess, is labor intensive, and is definitely not on anyone's "healthy foods" list. Our oven-fried chicken, on the other hand, solves all those problems—and has a crunchy, savory seasoned crust that will knock your socks off!

Buttermilk is a beautiful thing. It acts as a brine, tenderizing the chicken. It also gives something for the breading to really adhere to, so it helps ensure a nice crunchy crust. Finally, it lends just a touch of tangy flavor.

We love roasted okra, which has a wonderful Southern vibe that goes with the rest of the meal—but we recognize that there are many okra haters out there. Feel free to substitute green beans: you'll need to roast them 20 minutes, then transfer them to a bowl. Reheat them as directed below for the okra.

**MAKES 4 SERVINGS**

1.  Combine the chicken and buttermilk in a bowl and let it stand at room temperature for 30 minutes. (You can refrigerate the chicken in the buttermilk for up to 24 hours before proceeding; just be sure to remove it from the buttermilk and bring it to room temperature for 30 minutes before cooking.)

2.  Position the oven racks in the center and lower third of the oven and preheat the oven to 425°F. Coat a sheet pan with cooking spray.

3.  Toss the okra with the oil and ¼ teaspoon of the salt; arrange on the sheet pan and roast, shaking the pan occasionally, until tender and lightly browned, 15 to 18 minutes. Transfer to a bowl. Place a wire rack on the sheet pan.

4.  Combine the garlic powder, paprika, ancho powder, cayenne, and remaining ½ teaspoon salt. Remove the chicken from the buttermilk, shake off the excess, and season with the mixture. Spread the panko on a plate. Working with 1 piece at a time, coat the chicken, pressing the panko firmly to help the breadcrumbs adhere. Transfer to the rack on the sheet pan. Lightly coat the chicken with cooking spray.

5. Bake the chicken on the center rack of the oven for 15 minutes.
6. Meanwhile, brush the corn with the softened butter and season with ¼ teaspoon of the salt. Wrap each ear tightly in a 12-inch-long sheet of foil.
7. Rotate the pan front to back and place the corn directly on the lower rack of the oven. Continue cooking until the breadcrumbs are browned and an instant-read thermometer inserted into the center of the largest piece of the breast registers 160°F, 20 to 22 minutes longer. In the last 2 minutes of cooking, add the okra to the pan to heat it through.

## THE INS AND OUTS OF A WHOLE CUT-UP CHICKEN

Here are three good reasons to buy a whole chicken and cut it up yourself:

1. It is less expensive.
2. You can freeze the back, ribs, and wings for soup.
3. And the best reason of all: When you buy a cut-up chicken, the parts are not necessarily all from one bird, which means you won't get matching sizes of thighs and breasts. We recently bought a package with one 8-ounce and one 4.5-ounce thigh. That makes cooking all the pieces to the right degree of doneness more challenging!

But we get it: sometimes it just seems like too much trouble. So if you use a package of cut-up chicken with wildly different sizes of parts, simply keep a more vigilant eye on the cooking times. Also, packaged cut-up chicken usually includes overly large breast pieces, which you will need to cut across in half (see "To Halve and Halve Not," page 27). If the wings are on the breasts, remove them and freeze them for soup or your next Super Bowl party.

Use an instant-read thermometer and remove the breasts from the heat when they reach 160°F. Thighs should cook to 170°F. The good news is that because breasts are thicker, they often reach 160°F right about the time the thighs hit 170°F.

The eight pieces of a whole cut-up chicken are:

2 thighs
4 breast meat pieces
2 drumsticks

# HOISIN-MARMALADE CHICKEN

2 scallions, chopped (about ⅓ cup)

1 tablespoon grated fresh ginger

1 tablespoon lower-sodium soy sauce

2 teaspoons toasted sesame oil

1 (4-pound) chicken, cut into 8 pieces (see page 55)

1 cup long-grain white rice

¾ teaspoon salt, divided

3 carrots, peeled and cut diagonally into ½-inch-thick slices (about 1½ cups)

1 tablespoon plus 2 teaspoons canola oil, divided

4 baby bok choy, trimmed at the stem end and halved lengthwise

⅓ cup hoisin sauce

¼ cup orange marmalade

SHEET PAN
CUT-UP CHICKEN

This is a riff on a dish we call Five-Ingredient Chicken that we made regularly when the kids were little. It has a no-brainer sauce that delivers the perfect crowd-pleasing balance of sweet, salty, bitter, and sour, thanks to the unlikely combination of orange marmalade and hoisin sauce.

In this version we are using a whole cut-up chicken, but you could certainly make it with all thighs or breasts. (Just use internal temperature as your guide for cooking time: breasts should register 160°F and thighs 170°F.)

**MAKES 4 SERVINGS**

1. Preheat the oven to 425°F. Coat a sheet pan with cooking spray.
2. Combine the scallions, ginger, soy sauce, and sesame oil in a bowl; add the chicken and toss thoroughly. Let it stand at room temperature while you prepare the rice.
3. Spread the rice on the sheet pan. Combine 2¼ cups water and ¼ teaspoon of the salt and pour it over the rice. Bake for 15 minutes.
4. Meanwhile, combine the carrots, 2 teaspoons of the canola oil, and ¼ teaspoon of the salt in a large bowl.
5. After the rice has cooked for 15 minutes, give it a stir and smooth it into an even layer. Top it with the carrots and the chicken and roast for 20 minutes.
6. Meanwhile, add the bok choy to the now-empty large bowl and toss with the remaining 1 tablespoon oil and ¼ teaspoon salt. Combine the hoisin sauce and orange marmalade in a small bowl.
7. After it has roasted 20 minutes, brush the chicken with half the hoisin mixture. Place the bok choy halves, cut side down, on the pan and roast for 10 minutes. Brush the chicken with the remaining hoisin mixture and roast until an instant-read thermometer inserted into the center of the largest piece of the breast registers 160°F, 10 to 12 minutes more.

# HARISSA CHICKEN

3 tablespoons harissa sauce

3 tablespoons extra virgin olive oil, divided

2 teaspoons ground cumin

2 teaspoons grated orange zest

½ teaspoon ground cinnamon

1¼ teaspoons salt, divided

1 (4-pound) chicken, cut into 8 pieces (see page 55)

1 cup quinoa, rinsed

6 cups cauliflower florets (about 1¼ pounds)

1 cup red seedless grapes, halved

1 tablespoon coarsely chopped fresh cilantro

1 tablespoon coarsely chopped fresh mint

SHEET PAN
CUT-UP CHICKEN

Harissa sauce or paste is a North African condiment made from smoked chiles, garlic, spices, and olive oil. It packs a lot of heat—but also flavor beyond the heat, thanks to the smokiness of the chiles and the combination of spices, which usually includes caraway, coriander, and cumin seeds (and often many others).

We love the balance of the smoky heat with little bursts of sweet from the grapes. Cauliflower adds a nice earthy touch.

The chicken can marinate for up to 24 hours, or just while the quinoa cooks. After 20 minutes, it will seem as though the quinoa is ready, but the chicken and vegetables that you then place on top of it give off a lot of liquid. The quinoa absorbs the liquid—which gives it great flavor.

While this meal requires nearly an hour of cooking time, there is less than 10 minutes of active prep.

MAKES 4 SERVINGS

1. Preheat the oven to 425°F. Coat a sheet pan with cooking spray.

2. Combine the harissa, 2 tablespoons of the oil, the cumin, orange zest, cinnamon, and ½ teaspoon of the salt in a large bowl. Add the chicken and toss well to coat. Let it stand at room temperature while you proceed with the recipe.

3. Combine the quinoa, 3½ cups water, and ½ teaspoon of the salt on the sheet pan. Bake for 20 minutes.

4. Meanwhile, combine the cauliflower, grapes, and remaining 1 tablespoon oil in a bowl. Toss with the remaining ¼ teaspoon salt.

5. After 20 minutes, remove the quinoa from the oven and top with the chicken, cauliflower, and grapes. Return to the oven and bake until an instant-read thermometer inserted into the center of the largest piece of the breast registers 160°F, 33 to 35 minutes. Sprinkle with the cilantro and mint before serving.

# CORIANDER-CRUSTED WHOLE ROAST CHICKEN

1 (4-pound) whole chicken

1 pound beets, trimmed, peeled, and cut into ½-inch-thick wedges

2 tablespoons extra virgin olive oil, divided

1 tablespoon balsamic vinegar

2 teaspoons sugar

½ teaspoon salt, divided

¼ teaspoon ground black pepper, divided

2 fresh rosemary sprigs

Coriander Herb Crust (recipe follows)

1 lemon, halved

1 pound sweet potatoes (about 2 medium), peeled and cut into 1-inch chunks

SHEET PAN
WHOLE CHICKEN

Every home cook needs at least one really great whole roast chicken recipe in her/his repertoire. The goal is to get beautiful golden-brown crisp skin and tender, moist meat.

Many people erroneously believe that constant basting helps crisp the skin, and that is just not true. At the very end of cooking, when the pan juices have lots of fat, a quick brush on the skin can enhance the crispness, but when you baste early on, you use pan juices that are mostly the meat drippings, not fat. When you baste with anything other than the fat, you are simply moistening the skin, not crisping it.

The key to crisp skin starts before the bird goes in the oven. Let it stand at room temperature, uncovered, for 30 minutes. (Better yet, if you have the time, room, and foresight, let the chicken stand, uncovered, in the refrigerator overnight.) This dries the skin—and the less moisture, the crisper the skin gets when cooked.

In the meal below, we roast the beets in a foil packet to prevent the color from bleeding onto everything else.

**MAKES 4 SERVINGS**

1. Let the chicken stand, uncovered, at room temperature for 30 minutes.
2. Preheat the oven to 400°F. Coat a sheet pan with cooking spray.
3. Combine the beets with 1 tablespoon of the oil, vinegar, sugar, ¼ teaspoon of the salt, and ⅛ teaspoon of the pepper. Place them on half of a 24-inch-long sheet of heavy-duty foil (or double up if you use regular foil) and top with the rosemary sprigs. Fold the foil over the beets and crimp the edges tightly to seal.
4. Pat the chicken dry with paper towels. Pat the coriander crust (see opposite) over the chicken and place the lemon halves inside the chicken cavity. Tuck the wings back under the chicken and tie the drumsticks together using kitchen twine. Place on the sheet pan with the beet packet and roast for 50 minutes.

5. Meanwhile, combine the sweet potatoes with the remaining 1 tablespoon oil in a bowl. Toss with the remaining ¼ teaspoon salt and ⅛ teaspoon pepper.

6. After the chicken has roasted 50 minutes, spread the sweet potatoes out on the pan and roast until the vegetables are tender and an instant-read thermometer inserted into the thickest part of the thigh registers 170°F, 23 to 25 minutes longer.

7. Remove the pan from the oven and let the chicken rest for 10 minutes before carving.

## CORIANDER HERB CRUST

½ cup cilantro leaves, chopped

2 tablespoons extra virgin olive oil

Grated zest of 1 lemon

2 teaspoons ground cumin

1 teaspoon garlic powder

½ teaspoon salt

¼ teaspoon ground black pepper

Combine the ingredients in a large bowl.

### BEWARE THE PITH!

We love our Microplane grater for zesting, but here's an important tip: hold the fruit beneath the grating plane so you can see how deep into the peel you are going. You should never grate down as far as the white, which is the bitter pith. Also, keep in mind it is always easier to zest a whole fruit before you cut it up.

When using a Microplane grater with cheese and nutmeg, you can slide the food back and forth *on top* of the grater, because you don't need to see what is happening to the grated surface.

CORIANDER-CRUSTED WHOLE ROAST CHICKEN  62

# ROSEMARY SPATCHCOCK CHICKEN

BABY POTATOES + ASPARAGUS

3 tablespoons olive oil, divided

1 (4-pound) whole chicken

1¼ teaspoons salt, divided

½ teaspoon ground black pepper, divided

¼ cup fresh lemon juice

¼ cup unsalted chicken broth

1 tablespoon chopped fresh rosemary, plus 5 fresh rosemary sprigs

1 pound baby potatoes, quartered

1 pound asparagus, trimmed

SKILLET
WHOLE CHICKEN

This is one of our absolute favorite ways to cook chicken. It is stunning looking, which is lovely but not the main advantage: the skin gets crisp and brown, the meat is tender and juicy—and dinner is ready far more quickly than if you kept the chicken whole.

Don't be put off by the idea of cutting the bird like this—it is as easy as using kitchen shears or a knife to cut along each side of the backbone to remove it. Then you simply open the bird up like it is a book. It is that easy! (We freeze the backbones in a zip-top plastic bag to use in chicken soup.)

Besides the perfect chicken, our other favorite thing about this dish is what happens to the potatoes. Half of them come out with crisp, browned exteriors and creamy soft centers; the other half soak up all the delicious pan juices.

**MAKES 4 SERVINGS**

1. Preheat the oven to 425°F. Rub 1 tablespoon of the oil over the entire inside surface (including the sides) of a large ovenproof skillet.
2. To spatchcock the chicken, you need to first remove the backbone. Place the chicken, breast side down, on your work surface. Use kitchen shears or a knife to cut lengthwise along either side of the backbone to remove it. (Discard the bone, or freeze it for stock.) Open the chicken up like a book. While it is lying skin side facing down on your work surface, score the white cartilage that runs down the center (do not cut through to the meat) so the chicken lies perfectly flat. (Sometimes you need only cut through the little bit of cartilage at the end near the neck for it to lie flat.) Flip the bird over and season the skin with ½ teaspoon of the salt and ¼ teaspoon of the pepper.
3. Heat 1 tablespoon of the oil in the skillet over medium-high heat. When it is very hot, place the bird, skin side down, in the skillet. Season the surface facing up (the inside of the bird) with ½ teaspoon

*(recipe continues on page 68)*

of the salt and ⅛ teaspoon of the pepper. Press the chicken down with a spatula so that as much of the skin touches the pan surface as possible. Cook the chicken without moving it until it no longer sticks to the pan surface and is a lovely golden color on the underside, 8 to 10 minutes. Use two large spatulas to gently lift the bird out of the pan and transfer it to a plate.

4. Add the lemon juice, chicken broth, and chopped rosemary to the skillet and cook, stirring and scraping up any browned bits from the bottom of the pan, until the liquid is reduced by half and is somewhat milky looking, 1 to 2 minutes; remove from the heat.

5. Combine the potatoes with the remaining 1 tablespoon oil in a bowl. Toss with the remaining ¼ teaspoon salt and ⅛ teaspoon pepper and add half of them to the skillet. Return the chicken to the skillet, with the skin side facing up, and add the remaining potatoes and the rosemary sprigs on and around the chicken. Transfer to the oven and roast for 20 minutes.

6. Add the asparagus to the pan and continue roasting until an instant-read thermometer inserted into the thickest part of the thigh registers 170°F and the vegetables are cooked through, about 15 minutes longer.

## SPATCHCOCK: WE JUST LOVE SAYING THE WORD

We know, it almost sounds dirty. Spatchcock (see? We just said it again) may come from the old Irish phrase to "dispatch the cock," meaning make it more quickly when you split the bird down the middle, open it up, and lay it out flat on the grill.

You don't have to grill a spatchcocked bird—we cook ours in the oven. (We've done turkeys this way, too.) This may be more grammar than you care about, but as long as we are focusing on the word itself, it is worth noting that spatchcock can be a noun (the spatchcock is in the oven) or a verb (I spatchcocked that bird!). But you just watch: no matter how you use it, when you say it, people around you (and not just twelve-year-old boys) will get a funny smirky expression on their faces.

# TURKEY CHORIZO TACOS

1 small jicama (12 ounces), peeled and cut into ¼-inch-thick strips (about 2 cups)

5 large radishes, halved and thinly sliced

1 plum tomato, seeded and thinly sliced (about ½ cup)

1 serrano pepper, seeded and finely chopped

2 tablespoons chopped fresh cilantro

2 tablespoons fresh lime juice

¼ teaspoon salt

2 tablespoons olive oil

1 large white onion, cut into ¼-inch pieces (about 2 cups)

2 links cured chorizo sausage (4 ounces), halved lengthwise and thinly sliced across

3 garlic cloves, minced

1½ pounds turkey cutlets, cut across into ¼-inch-thick strips

1 teaspoon ancho chile powder

½ teaspoon salt

12 corn tortillas

SKILLET
TURKEY CUTLETS

Chorizo lends its signature meaty, smoky flavor to the tacos— and a little goes a long way. Be sure to used *cured* chorizo, not fresh: the cured is already cooked through and has a drier texture. Ancho chile powder, which is sold with other spices in the grocery store, adds a little fruity heat.

The salad is the perfect counterpoint to the big bold swaggering flavors of the tacos.

**MAKES 4 SERVINGS**

1. Make the jicama-radish salad: Combine the jicama, radishes, tomato, serrano pepper, cilantro, lime juice, and salt in a bowl.
2. Heat the oil in a large skillet over medium-high heat. Add the onion and cook, stirring occasionally, until it starts to soften, about 2 minutes. Stir in the chorizo and garlic and cook until the garlic is somewhat softened, about 2 minutes. Add the turkey, ancho powder, and salt and cook, stirring occasionally, until the turkey is cooked through, 3 to 4 minutes. Remove the pan from the heat and cover to keep warm.
3. Warm the tortillas, one at a time, directly over a medium flame on a gas stove, turning frequently, until heated and browned in spots, about 1 minute, or in the microwave according to the package directions. Stack the warmed tortillas on a plate and drape them with a kitchen towel to keep them warm and pliable.
4. Serve the tortillas as is and invite diners to build their own tacos, or fill each tortilla with the chorizo-turkey mixture and salad, fold it in half, and serve them ready to eat.

### SERRANO VERSUS JALAPEÑO
*Serrano and jalapeño peppers are nearly the same size and shape; serranos tend to be a little longer and thinner. Though not usually wildly hot, serranos are nonetheless about three times hotter than jalapeños. But proceed with caution: every once in a while you get a super fiery one.*

# NOT YOUR MOMMA'S SLOPPY JOES

1 tablespoon olive oil

1 medium red onion, finely chopped (about 1 cup)

6 ounces white mushrooms, finely chopped

2 garlic cloves, minced

¼ teaspoon salt

1 small zucchini (about 6 ounces), finely diced (about 1 cup)

½ orange or red bell pepper, finely diced (about ½ cup)

12 ounces lean ground turkey

⅔ cup ketchup

2 tablespoons harissa sauce

2 tablespoons lightly packed light brown sugar

1½ teaspoons ground coriander

½ teaspoon ground cumin

¼ teaspoon ground cinnamon

4 potato sandwich rolls

SKILLET
GROUND TURKEY

We have nothing against the classic Sloppy Joe, but we wanted to update it with aromatic spices and a little bit of heat. Our criterion for any new version, though, was that it had to still be both weeknight and game-day friendly—and deliver lots of vegetable power without detracting from the juicy, messy goodness for which this all-American sandwich is known.

Mission accomplished: the end result is as fast and easy to cook as ever—but it also includes zucchini, bell pepper, and mushrooms and the irresistible combination of ground coriander, cumin, and (a touch of) cinnamon. Harissa sauce adds even more spices, along with a kick. (You can adjust the amount of harissa to suit your heat tolerance or omit it altogether.)

**MAKES 4 SERVINGS**

1. Heat the oil in a large skillet over medium-high heat. Add the onion, mushrooms, garlic, and salt and cook, stirring occasionally, until the liquid from the mushrooms is absorbed, about 4 minutes. Add the zucchini and bell pepper and cook until the vegetables are tender, about 5 minutes.

2. Add the turkey and cook, breaking it into smaller pieces with a wooden spoon, until it is cooked through, about 5 minutes. Stir in the ketchup, harissa, brown sugar, coriander, cumin, and cinnamon and cook until thickened, about 3 minutes.

3. Divide the mixture among the rolls and serve.

## AS SWEET AS . . . KETCHUP?!?

Here is a mind-blowing fact: Ounce for ounce, ketchup has more sugar than ice cream. In fact, ketchup contains 25 percent sugar. When David puts his typical 2 to 4 tablespoons of ketchup on his burger, he adds between 8 and 16 grams of sugar—half a cup of ice cream's worth!

Don't despair—there are new, very good lower-sugar (and still kid-friendly) options, like True Made Foods ketchup, which gets a lot of its sweet flavor from butternut squash and carrots. But read labels carefully, because there are also some tricky products out in the marketplace that proudly proclaim they have "no added sugar," but are made with sucralose, an artificial sweetener.

# TURKEY-MANGO STIR-FRY WITH CASHEWS

**1½ pounds turkey cutlets, cut into 1-inch pieces**

**½ teaspoon salt**

**¼ teaspoon ground black pepper**

**2 tablespoons canola oil, divided**

**1 medium red onion, cut into ½-inch pieces (about 1 cup)**

**6 ounces shiitake mushrooms, stems discarded and caps thinly sliced**

**3 garlic cloves, minced**

**1 tablespoon minced fresh ginger**

**4 ounces snow peas**

**1 large mango (about 14 ounces), peeled, pitted, and cut into ¾-inch cubes**

**2 tablespoons fresh lime juice**

**2 tablespoons sugar**

**1 tablespoon sriracha sauce**

**1 tablespoon fish sauce**

**⅓ cup salted roasted cashews**

**2 (10-ounce) bags frozen white or brown rice**

SKILLET
TURKEY CUTLETS

Juicy sweet mango and cashews make this simple stir-fry a kid-friendly meal. If you have a mixed crowd—some who like it spicy and some who do not—leave the sriracha out entirely and bring the bottle to the table for diners to use as they see fit.

This is not a typical cornstarch-thickened stir-fry sauce: the bright lime juice and deep umami-laden fish sauce serve as supporting players, subtly enhancing the clean, fresh flavors of the turkey, mango, and crisp snow peas.

**MAKES 4 SERVINGS**

1. Combine the turkey, salt, and pepper in a bowl.
2. Heat 1 tablespoon of the oil in a large skillet over medium-high heat. Add half of the turkey and cook, stirring occasionally, until lightly browned and no longer pink, 3 to 4 minutes; transfer to a plate. Add the remaining turkey to the pan and again cook until it is no longer pink, 3 to 4 minutes.
3. Heat the remaining 1 tablespoon oil in the skillet over medium-high heat. Add the onion and mushrooms and cook, stirring occasionally, until slightly softened, 3 to 4 minutes. Stir in the garlic and ginger and cook until fragrant, about 1 minute. Add the snow peas and cook, stirring, until bright green, about 1 minute. Add the reserved turkey, any of its juices that have accumulated on the plate, and the mango and cook for 2 minutes. Stir in the lime juice, sugar, sriracha, and fish sauce and cook, stirring, until heated through and well distributed, about 1 minute. Remove from the heat and stir in the cashews.
4. Microwave the rice according to package directions. Serve the stir-fry over the rice.

## FROZEN AND/OR MICROWAVABLE RICE

In the past few years, a number of frozen cooked rice products have come on the market—as have a slew of shelf-stable, microwavable versions. Our first criterion for choosing a cooked rice we'll use is what it says on the package label. If it contains anything other than rice and salt, we're not interested. (And we prefer no salt, but that is hard to come by.) That rules out the vast majority of shelf-stable microwavable products; most have fat, seasoning, and odd unpronounceable ingredients added.

You are likely to find a number of good, clean choices in the freezer section of your grocery store. We also make extra when we cook rice, and keep that in the freezer. Whichever way you go, it makes life (and by life, we mean cleanup) a lot easier when you have cooked rice on hand.

# GEMELLI WITH TURKEY SAUSAGE, SPINACH, AND ASIAGO

2 tablespoons extra virgin olive oil

12 ounces Italian turkey sausage, removed from the casings

1 medium onion, chopped (about 1 cup)

8 garlic cloves, thinly sliced

8 ounces gemelli pasta

2 pints grape tomatoes, halved

½ teaspoon salt

1 (5-ounce) package baby spinach (about 6 cups)

½ cup shredded aged Asiago cheese, plus more for serving

⅓ cup fresh basil leaves, thinly sliced

¼ teaspoon ground black pepper

SKILLET
TURKEY SAUSAGE

It is amazing what happens to pasta when it is cooked in flavored liquid rather than plain water. In this simple dish, turkey sausage and cherry tomatoes, which burst open as they simmer, give the pasta robust flavor. This is one of those go-to, never-fail recipes you can whip up on the spur of the moment.

**MAKES 4 SERVINGS**

1. Heat the oil in a large skillet over medium heat. Add the sausage and onion and cook, breaking the sausage into smaller pieces with a wooden spoon, until the onion is translucent and the sausage is lightly browned, 10 to 11 minutes. Stir in the garlic and cook until it is tender and golden, 3 to 4 minutes.

2. Increase the heat to medium-high. Add the pasta, tomatoes, salt, and 4 cups water. Cook, stirring often, until the pasta is tender and the liquid has thickened, 18 to 20 minutes. Add the spinach and cook until just wilted, about 1 minute. Remove from the heat and stir in the Asiago, basil, and pepper. Serve with additional Asiago at the table.

## SAUSAGE SHOWDOWN

Sausage certainly isn't a health food, but it has great flavor. We use healthier turkey sausage for our "everyday" meals and splurge now and then on pork sausage. While exact numbers will vary by brand, we compared labels of two grocery-store brands. We adjusted the size to make the nutrition numbers comparable: these numbers are for about 3.2 ounces. (That's typically one turkey sausage link, or about one and a quarter of the smaller pork links.)

| | PORK SAUSAGE | TURKEY SAUSAGE |
|---|---|---|
| Calories | 288 | 160 |
| Fat (g) | 21 | 9 |
| Saturated fat (g) | 8 | 2.5 |
| Sodium (mg) | 638 | 640 |
| Sugar (g) | 2.5 | 1 |
| Protein | 17.5 | 16 |

# WEEKNIGHT HERB-ROASTED TURKEY BREAST

4 medium carrots, peeled and halved lengthwise

4 small parsnips (about 1 pound), peeled and halved lengthwise

1 pound baby Yukon Gold potatoes, halved

8 shallots, peeled

1 tablespoon olive oil

½ teaspoon salt

¼ teaspoon ground black pepper

### ANCHOVY-HERB RUB

2 tablespoons olive oil

2 oil-packed anchovy fillets, drained, mashed to a paste with a fork

2 teaspoons chopped fresh sage

1 teaspoon chopped fresh thyme

1 teaspoon garlic powder

¾ teaspoon salt

¼ teaspoon ground black pepper

1 (2½-pound) bone-in turkey breast half

### SHEET PAN
TURKEY BREAST

Turkey is not just for Thanksgiving. We roast turkey breasts year-round—often with the plan of having leftovers for lunches and other dinners. (Or to stir into risotto, page 248; or add to Skillet Lasagna with Caramelized Onions and Spinach, page 231; or to make Orzo with Pan-Roasted Cherry Tomatoes, Olives, and Feta, page 224, more hefty.)

This meal couldn't be simpler: you make a paste with mashed anchovies and seasoning that gets rubbed on the breast, surround the turkey with carrots, potatoes, parsnips, and shallots, and stick it in the oven.

If you've never had roasted parsnips or shallots, you're in for a treat. Parsnips get an almost haunting earthy-sweet nuttiness to them, while shallots get that classic caramelized oniony flavor. We love these roasted vegetables so much that we make them on their own as a side dish. They are great for fall gatherings because they can be made in advance and reheated.

**MAKES 4 TO 6 SERVINGS**

1. Preheat the oven to 425°F. Coat a sheet pan with cooking spray.
2. Combine the carrots, parsnips, potatoes, shallots, and oil in a large bowl. Toss with the salt and pepper.
3. Make the rub: Combine the oil, anchovy paste, sage, thyme, garlic powder, salt, and pepper to form a paste in a small bowl. Pat the turkey breast dry with paper towels and rub the paste over the entire surface.
4. Place the turkey in the center of the sheet pan and arrange the vegetables around it. Roast it until an instant-read thermometer inserted into the center of the breast registers 160°F and the vegetables are tender, 55 to 60 minutes. Remove from the oven and let the turkey rest 5 to 10 minutes before slicing.

## FOR THE LOVE—OR HATE—OF ANCHOVIES

We have a friend who calls bottled anchovies "little mustaches." We get it: the tiny little bones can feel a little furry in your mouth. Certainly the assertive fishy taste turns a lot of people off. But here's the thing: no one ever said you had to eat them whole, straight out of the jar. They are often minced into sauces, dressings, and so on, where they add incredible savory depth—often when you can't even discern they are there. Fish sauce used in Asian cuisine works in much the same way: you wouldn't down a spoonful on its own, but it transforms dishes with its umami presence.

# DUCK BREASTS WITH CRANBERRY-RED WINE SAUCE

4 (6-ounce) boneless, skin-on duck breast halves

1 teaspoon salt, divided

½ teaspoon ground black pepper, divided

2 tablespoons olive oil, divided

1 pound fingerling potatoes, quartered lengthwise

12 ounces Brussels sprouts, halved

1 medium shallot, finely chopped (about 3 tablespoons)

¼ cup dried cranberries

½ cup unsalted chicken broth

⅓ cup dry red wine, such as Zinfandel

4 teaspoons sugar

1 teaspoon raspberry vinegar

2 tablespoons unsalted butter

SKILLET
DUCK BREASTS

Why don't Americans eat more duck? It's the bird that eats like meat—but has the good, lean nutrition of chicken (see opposite). What's more, duck breasts are actually easier to cook than chicken breasts, because they don't dry out as much.

That's one reason (of many) we like to serve them when we entertain: they can be made ahead and gently reheated without getting dry. They are equally pleasing to people who don't eat red meat and people who do, and their deep flavor stands up to a variety of wonderful sauces, like this favorite of ours made from red wine and cranberries.

This is a very simple dinner to put together. For very little work, it is an elegant and truly delicious meal.

**MAKES 4 SERVINGS**

1. Preheat the oven to 425°F.

2. With a sharp knife, score the skin on each duck breast into a crosshatch pattern, taking care to cut down to the flesh but not through it. (This helps release the fat under the skin, allowing it to form a beautiful honey-brown crisp crust.) Season the duck with ½ teaspoon of the salt and ¼ teaspoon of the pepper.

3. Heat 1 tablespoon of the oil in a large ovenproof skillet over medium heat. Add the potatoes and ⅛ teaspoon of the salt and cook, stirring occasionally, until they begin to brown, 4 to 5 minutes. Transfer the skillet to the oven and roast the potatoes for 5 minutes.

4. Meanwhile, toss the Brussels sprouts with the remaining 1 tablespoon oil, ⅛ teaspoon of the salt, and ⅛ teaspoon of the pepper.

5. Add the Brussels sprouts to the skillet with the potatoes and cook until the vegetables are nearly but not fully cooked through, 10 to 12 minutes. Remove the skillet from the oven and transfer the vegetables to a bowl. Leave the oven on.

6. Heat the skillet over medium heat, add the duck, skin side down, and cook until well browned, 4 to 5 minutes. If there is more than

2 tablespoons of fat in the skillet, remove it with a spoon. Flip the duck over, return the potatoes and Brussels sprouts to the skillet, place in the oven, and roast until an instant-read thermometer inserted horizontally into the center of a duck breast registers 135°F (the temperature will continue to rise another 5 to 7 degrees after it is removed from the oven), 5 to 6 minutes. Remove the pan from the oven, transfer the vegetables to a bowl or platter, and drape them loosely with foil to keep warm. Place the duck on a cutting board, tent with foil, and let it rest 5 minutes.

7. Meanwhile, heat the skillet over medium-high heat. Add the shallot and cranberries and cook, stirring, for 1 minute. Add the chicken broth, wine, sugar, and vinegar; bring to a boil and cook until reduced by about two-thirds and starting to thicken, 3 to 3½ minutes. Remove from the heat and swirl in the butter until melted. Season with the remaining ¼ teaspoon salt and ⅛ teaspoon pepper.

8. To serve, cut the duck across into thin slices. Divide among four plates, fanning the slices, and spoon the sauce over the slices. Serve with the potatoes and Brussels sprouts.

## DUCK MATH

Duck is much leaner than most people assume. The chart shows how 3 ounces of cooked duck (we used Pekin, the most common breed) stacks up against the same portion of chicken breast.

According to some food scientists (and nearly all chefs), duck is actually red meat and should be cooked as such. In other words, unlike chicken, duck is often served and consumed pink in the center. Duck does not carry the same risk of salmonella that chicken does—but it is not at zero risk, either. So if you are pregnant or immune compromised, you'll probably want your duck (and all meats) cooked to 160°F. Everyone else might consider eating duck the way you would a medium steak: cooked to 140°F, at which point it will be pink and juicy.

| | PEKIN DUCK | | CHICKEN BREAST | |
| --- | --- | --- | --- | --- |
| | SKIN ON | SKINLESS | SKIN ON | SKINLESS |
| Calories | 172 | 119 | 167 | 128 |
| Protein | 21g | 24g | 25g | 26g |
| Fat | 9g | 2g | 7g | 3g |
| Saturated Fat | 2g | 1g | 2g | 1g |

# MOROCCAN CORNISH HENS

1 navel orange, unpeeled, cut into 8 rounds

1 cup pitted Medjool dates (about 4 ounces)

4 garlic cloves, minced

1 cup fresh cilantro leaves, finely chopped

1 teaspoon ground cumin

¼ teaspoon ground cardamom

¼ teaspoon ground coriander

¾ teaspoon salt, divided

2 Cornish hens

⅓ cup pimiento-stuffed green olives

6 tablespoons balsamic vinegar

6 tablespoons Marsala wine

3 tablespoons honey

6 cups broccoli florets (about 1¼ pounds)

1 tablespoon olive oil

ORANGE COUSCOUS

½ cup orange juice

¼ teaspoon salt

1 cup couscous

SHEET PAN
CORNISH HENS

This is everything a dish for entertaining should be: it can be made well ahead, has the universally appealing flavor combination of salty and sweet, and it is absolutely beautiful whether you serve it individually plated or on a platter. Because each person is served half a hen, they get both dark and light meat—which means everyone gets what they prefer.

For a beautiful presentation, serve the hens on top of the orange slices, letting the oranges peek out from underneath; spoon the sauce over the hens and sprinkle the platter with the dates and olives.

**MAKES 4 SERVINGS**

1. Preheat the oven to 425°F. Coat a sheet pan with cooking spray.
2. Arrange the orange slices on the sheet pan and place the dates on top of the oranges.
3. Combine the garlic, cilantro, cumin, cardamom, coriander, and ½ teaspoon of the salt in a small bowl.
4. To cut the hens in half, start by slicing lengthwise along each side of the backbone and remove it. Open the hen up like a book and cut lengthwise along the side of the breastbone. Place each hen half, skin side up, on top of two orange slices (the slices will stick out at the ends) and pat the cilantro mixture evenly over the entire top surface of the hens. Be sure that all of the dates are tucked under the hens— if they are left exposed, they will scorch. Sprinkle the olives on the sheet pan.
5. Whisk the vinegar, Marsala, and honey in a bowl until the honey is dissolved; pour over the hens. (The hens may be made up to this point, wrapped in plastic and refrigerated, for 1 to 2 days. Bring them to room temperature before cooking.) Roast the hens for 20 minutes.
6. Meanwhile, toss the broccoli with the olive oil and a ¼ teaspoon of the salt.

7. When the hens have roasted for 20 minutes, add the broccoli to the pan and roast until an instant-read thermometer inserted into the center of the breast registers 160°F, about 15 minutes more.

8. Meanwhile, make the orange couscous: Combine the orange juice, salt, and ¾ cup water in a medium bowl and microwave on high until nearly boiling. Stir in the couscous, cover, and set aside for 5 minutes until the liquid is fully absorbed.

9. To serve, scrape the couscous out of the bowl with the tines of a fork (this keeps it fluffy). Place two orange slices on each plate and top with a hen half; spoon the pan sauce over the hens and serve with the broccoli.

## KNOW YOUR BIRDS

- **CORNISH HEN** (aka Cornish game hen, Rock Cornish game hen): simply a small, young chicken, younger than 5 weeks old and under 2 pounds

- **BROILER/FRYER:** younger than 10 weeks old and over 3 or 4 pounds

- **ROASTER/ROASTING CHICKEN:** 8 to 10 weeks old and over 5 pounds

- **CAPON:** neutered male chicken that is less than 4 months old

MOROCCAN CORNISH HENS   84

# 2

# BEEF, PORK, AND LAMB

## COOKING RED MEAT

To ensure you eke out the most, best flavor from meat, you need to choose the right cooking method for the cut and cook it to the ideal degree of doneness (temperature). For many cuts, you have choices: several cooking methods and more than one degree of doneness that can bring out the best flavor and texture.

Bear in mind that meat is almost always at its most flavorful and tender when cooked a very short time (to medium-rare, or at least pink in the center) or a very long time (like a brisket or pot roast).

## ROAST

When you cook meat with little or no liquid on a sheet pan, you are roasting it. To roast is to surround the food with dry heat, which allows it to cook from all directions. This is the quintessential sheet-pan method and it is ideal for larger cuts, like beef or pork tenderloin.

Roasting and baking are the same thing, though they are used slightly differently. You wouldn't say "I am going to roast cookies" any more than you would say "I baked the prime rib."

## BRAISE/STEW

To braise is to cook partially immersed in liquid. It is typically done at a lower heat and for a longer period of time. Of course, the bigger the cut of meat, the longer the braise. It works particularly well with tougher, leaner cuts (like the lamb shanks on page 144) that benefit from cooking until they are falling-off-the-bone tender.

We often brown (sear) meat before braising to give it additional flavor. We may braise it either on top of the stove or in the oven.

## STIR-FRY

This term has come to mean cooking bite-size (usually boneless) pieces over high stovetop heat and keeping it moving in the pan. We stir-fry strips, 1-inch chunks, or ground meat.

## SEAR

Chops and steaks get their irresistible brown crust when you place them in a hot pan and let them sit without moving. Thicker cuts may be seared and finished in the oven (roasted) to ensure the interior gets cooked to the desired degree of doneness without scorching the exterior. Meat that is less than about 1½ inches thick can be cooked all the way through by searing each side over medium-high heat.

Pat off any excess moisture from meat and bring it to room temperature before you sear it. Give it space in the pan—if it is too crowded, the meat will steam rather than sear.

## BROIL

This is essentially upside-down grilling. When you broil, direct heat (not through a pan surface) cooks the meat from above, which can brown the top but leaves the interior medium-rare. It is best for thinner cuts, like London broil, flank, and skirt steaks, or when you want to add exterior browning at the end of cooking larger cuts.

### TEMPERATURE GUIDE FOR RED MEAT

**RARE**: 120°F to 125°F
**MEDIUM-RARE**: 130°F to 135°F
**MEDIUM**: 140°F to 145°F
**MEDIUM-WELL**: 145°F to 150°F
**WELL-DONE**: 155°F and up
**GROUND MEAT**: 165°F

# RIGATONI WITH MEAT SAUCE

2 tablespoons extra virgin olive oil

1 medium onion, finely diced (about 1 cup)

1 medium carrot, peeled and finely chopped (about ⅓ cup)

1 celery stalk, finely chopped (about ⅓ cup)

1 tablespoon chopped fresh oregano or 1 teaspoon dried

12 ounces lean ground beef (85%)

5 garlic cloves, minced

½ cup dry red wine, such as Cabernet Sauvignon

1 (28-ounce) can crushed tomatoes with basil

2 tablespoons tomato paste

1 medium zucchini (about 8 ounces), trimmed and cut into ½-inch dice (about 1¼ cups)

12 ounces rigatoni pasta

1 teaspoon salt

¼ teaspoon ground black pepper

½ cup grated Pecorino Romano cheese

⅓ cup fresh basil leaves, thinly sliced

SKILLET
GROUND BEEF

This is the hearty pasta dish that everyone loves to eat. It gets its stick-to-your-bones, deep, rich flavor from the ground beef cooked in red wine and a double hit of tomatoes. We use canned crushed tomatoes to give the sauce body and tomato paste for intensity.

The diced zucchini melds into the sauce and adds texture and heft to the meat (and more vegetable nutrients).

As with all heroic pasta dishes, the rigatoni cooks right in the sauce, which not only saves you from having to wash an extra pan—it makes the pasta more flavorful.

Serve this with a green salad. We like ours dressed with the Shallot Vinaigrette (recipe follows).

**MAKES 4 SERVINGS**

1. Heat the oil in a large skillet over medium heat. Add the onion, carrot, celery, and oregano and cook, stirring occasionally, until slightly softened, 4 to 5 minutes. Add the beef and garlic and cook, breaking the beef into smaller pieces with a wooden spoon, until the onion and beef are lightly browned, 9 to 10 minutes. Pour in the wine and cook until it is nearly evaporated, 1 to 2 minutes. Add the crushed tomatoes, tomato paste, and zucchini; bring to a simmer and cook, stirring often, until slightly thickened, 2 minutes.

2. Stir in the rigatoni, salt, pepper, and 3 cups water; bring to a simmer and cook, stirring often, until the sauce is somewhat thickened, about 18 minutes. Add 1 cup water and continue cooking until the pasta is tender, 9 to 10 minutes more.

3. Serve the rigatoni topped with the Romano and basil.

## SHALLOT VINAIGRETTE

1 medium shallot,
finely chopped (about
2 tablespoons)

1 tablespoon red wine vinegar

2 teaspoons Dijon mustard

1 teaspoon honey

¼ teaspoon salt

⅛ teaspoon ground black
pepper

3 tablespoons extra virgin
olive oil

Combine the shallot, vinegar, mustard, honey, salt, and pepper in a
small bowl. Slowly whisk in the oil until combined.

# JUCY LUCYS

1½ pounds lean ground beef (85%)

1 teaspoon salt, divided

½ teaspoon ground black pepper, divided

4 slices (3 ounces) deli-sliced extra sharp Cheddar cheese, stacked and cut into a total of 16 equal-size pieces

3 tablespoons olive oil, divided

1 large Vidalia or other sweet onion, thinly sliced (about 2 cups)

3 garlic cloves, thinly sliced

1½ pounds Swiss chard, trimmed, center rib removed, and leaves torn into bite-size pieces (about 12 cups)

4 potato sandwich rolls

4 lettuce leaves (romaine, Boston)

4 beefsteak tomato slices

SKILLET
GROUND BEEF

Matt's is one of two rival bars in Minnesota that claim to have invented the Jucy Lucy, a burger made up of two thin beef patties that sandwich a layer of American cheese. The beauty of this burger is that when you seal the edges of the two patties around the cheese, it keeps the center really, well—juicy. American cheese gets creamier when it melts, but we prefer Cheddar for its more robust flavor and nonprocessed ingredients. (You can use any Cheddar, but deli slices make it easy to get a nice even thickness.)

We took some other liberties as well. We added meltingly sweet onions and a side of mild Swiss chard sautéed with garlic—and maybe a beer or two.

**MAKES 4 SERVINGS**

1. Gently mix the beef, ½ teaspoon of the salt, and ¼ teaspoon of the pepper in a bowl. Form the mixture into 8 thin patties 3½ to 4 inches wide. Place 4 of the patties on your work surface and top each with 4 pieces of the Cheddar, making sure you leave a border clear of cheese all the way around. Top with the remaining patties and firmly pinch the edges together to seal in the cheese.

2. Heat 1 tablespoon of the oil in a large skillet over medium-high heat. Add the onion and ¼ teaspoon of the salt and cook, stirring occasionally, until tender and golden brown, 9 to 10 minutes. Transfer to a bowl.

3. Reduce the heat to medium and add the remaining 2 tablespoons oil. Stir in the garlic and cook until it just begins to brown around the edges, about 45 seconds. Add the Swiss chard and the remaining ¼ teaspoon salt and ¼ teaspoon pepper. Cook, tossing occasionally, until the chard is wilted and tender, 4 to 5 minutes; transfer to a bowl.

4. Wipe the skillet with a paper towel to remove any moisture, return it to medium heat and add the patties. Cook, turning once, until they are browned and cooked through, 9 to 10 minutes.

5. Place the bottom half of each roll on a serving plate. Top each with a lettuce leaf, tomato slice, patty, and some of the onion; close the sandwiches. Let the burgers cool for 2 to 3 minutes before serving, because the cheese will be very hot.

6. Meanwhile, heat the skillet over medium-high heat. Return the chard to the pan and cook to heat through, about 1 minute. Serve the greens with the burgers.

# SPAGHETTI AND MEATBALLS

1¼ pounds lean ground beef (85%)

1 large egg

⅓ cup Italian-style dried breadcrumbs

⅓ cup grated Parmesan cheese

½ teaspoon salt, divided

½ teaspoon ground black pepper, divided

2 tablespoons olive oil, divided

1 medium onion, chopped (about 1 cup)

4 garlic cloves, minced

1 teaspoon dried basil

1 teaspoon dried oregano

1 (28-ounce) can crushed tomatoes

3 tablespoons tomato paste

8 ounces spaghetti

SKILLET
GROUND BEEF

This is the classic, beloved Mommy-food dinner—but made in just one pan. We think this one-pan method actually makes good old-fashioned spaghetti and meatballs even better because the spaghetti absorbs all the great sauce flavor. (Just don't tell your mom.)

The secret to really good meatballs is in how much you do or don't handle them. When forming the meatballs, it is easy to pack them too tight, which makes the meat tougher and drier. Of course, you have to compress them enough that they hold together, but chances are that requires less handling and compacting than you think.

MAKES 4 SERVINGS

1. Combine the beef, egg, breadcrumbs, Parmesan, ¼ teaspoon of the salt, and ¼ teaspoon of the pepper in a large bowl; mix well and form into 12 meatballs.

2. Heat 1 tablespoon of the oil in a large skillet over medium heat. Add the meatballs and cook, turning occasionally, until they are browned and nearly cooked through, 8 to 9 minutes; transfer to a plate.

3. Heat the remaining 1 tablespoon oil over medium heat. Add the onion and cook until the onion just begins to soften, 2 to 3 minutes. Stir in the garlic, basil, and oregano and cook for 2 minutes until the onion is softened and the garlic is no longer raw.

4. Increase the heat to medium-high; add the tomatoes, tomato paste, spaghetti, 3 cups water, and the remaining ¼ teaspoon salt and ¼ teaspoon pepper. Bring to a boil and cook, stirring often, until the spaghetti is almost cooked through, 12 to 13 minutes. Add the meatballs and continue cooking until the pasta is al dente and the meatballs are hot and cooked through, 5 to 6 minutes more.

# CLASSIC ALL-AMERICAN MEATLOAF

**CHEESY BROCCOLI + BAKED POTATOES**

4 (8-ounce) russet potatoes, scrubbed

2 pounds lean ground beef (85%)

1 medium onion, cut into ¼-inch dice (about 1 cup)

2 large eggs

¾ cup plain dried breadcrumbs

½ cup ketchup, divided

1 tablespoon yellow mustard

1½ teaspoons garlic powder

1 teaspoon dried oregano

¾ teaspoon dried thyme

1 teaspoon salt

½ teaspoon ground black pepper

6 cups broccoli florets (about 1¼ pounds)

1 tablespoon olive oil

2 ounces sharp Cheddar cheese, shredded

Softened butter or sour cream (optional)

SHEET PAN
GROUND BEEF

We mistakenly believed that meatloaf was created during the Great Depression as a way to extend the meaty pleasure of then-precious ground beef with inexpensive breadcrumbs and basic seasonings. Apparently the Romans had already had the idea in the fifth century. There are versions throughout the world—from the boiled meatloaf in Vietnam to the stuffed *pan de carne* in Argentina to the curried layered South African dish often baked with a custard-like topping. It became popular in the United States with the invention of the meat grinder in the late 1800s.

We can't help but love the classic version we grew up with—nor can we imagine a meatloaf without the ketchup glaze on top! We serve this with its BFFs: baked potatoes and cheesy broccoli. (Is there any other way?)

**MAKES 4 SERVINGS**

1.  Preheat the oven to 400°F. Line a sheet pan with foil and coat with cooking spray.

2.  Wrap each potato in a sheet of foil. Place in the oven directly on the rack, along the sides to leave room for the sheet pan. Bake the potatoes until they are tender when pierced with a fork, about 1 hour.

3.  Meanwhile, combine the beef, onion, eggs, breadcrumbs, ¼ cup of the ketchup, the mustard, garlic powder, oregano, thyme, salt, and pepper in a large bowl; mix well. Transfer the mixture to the prepared sheet pan and form into a 9 x 4 x 2-inch loaf. Spread the remaining ¼ cup ketchup over the meatloaf. Bake for 35 minutes.

4.  Toss the broccoli with the oil in a bowl. After the meatloaf has baked for 35 minutes, add the broccoli to the sheet pan and bake until an instant-read thermometer inserted into the center of the meatloaf registers 165°F and the broccoli is crisp-tender, about 20 minutes. Top the broccoli with the Cheddar and bake until the cheese melts, about 1 minute.

5.  Let the meatloaf rest for 5 minutes before slicing. Split each baked potato and serve with butter or sour cream, if desired.

# BEEF AND VEGETABLE STIR-FRY

6 ounces medium flat rice noodles (Pad Thai–style)

½ cup unsalted chicken broth

3 tablespoons hoisin sauce

2 teaspoons cornstarch

1 teaspoon chili-garlic sauce

2 tablespoons lower-sodium soy sauce, divided

2 tablespoons sake, divided

1 pound boneless sirloin steak, cut across into thin strips

3 tablespoons canola oil, divided

1 medium onion, cut into ½-inch dice (about 1 cup)

3 garlic cloves, minced

1 tablespoon minced fresh ginger

2 bell peppers, assorted colors, cut into thin strips

8 ounces sugar snap peas

2 baby bok choy (about 8 ounces), coarsely chopped

SKILLET
SIRLOIN

This vegetable-rich stir-fry is light-years healthier and fresher tasting than takeout could ever be . . . and it will be on your table faster than delivery. It gets the requisite fragrance and flavor from hoisin—the intensely flavored salty-sweet fermented sauce that enhances so many classic Chinese dishes. We chose red and yellow bell peppers, baby bok choy, and sugar snaps, but feel free to substitute other vegetables. (Adjust your cooking times accordingly.)

We've used beefy, slightly chewy sirloin steak; thinly sliced top round also works well. The thinner strips of top round are less chewy than sirloin but have a less robustly meaty flavor. If you don't have sake, you can either substitute white wine or leave it out entirely.

**MAKES 4 SERVINGS**

1. Fill a large skillet with water and bring to a boil over high heat. Add the noodles and cook according to package directions; drain and set aside.

2. Combine the chicken broth, hoisin sauce, cornstarch, chili-garlic sauce, 1 tablespoon of the soy sauce, and 1 tablespoon of the sake in a bowl.

3. Combine the steak with the remaining 1 tablespoon soy sauce and 1 tablespoon sake in a bowl.

4. Heat 1 tablespoon of the oil in the skillet over high heat. Add half of the beef and cook, stirring occasionally, until it just loses its pinkness, 3 to 4 minutes. Transfer the beef to a bowl and repeat with another 1 tablespoon oil and the remaining beef. Set the beef aside.

5. Heat the remaining 1 tablespoon oil in the skillet over high heat. Add the onion, garlic, and ginger and cook, stirring, until fragrant, about 1 minute. Stir in the bell peppers, sugar snap peas, and bok choy and cook until crisp-tender, 3 to 3½ minutes. Add the beef and cook for 1 minute to heat it through. Stir in the broth mixture, bring to a boil, and cook until the sauce thickens, about 1 minute. Serve over the noodles.

# BEEF AND ROOT VEGETABLE STEW

2 pounds beef chuck roast, trimmed and cut into 1-inch chunks

¾ teaspoon salt, divided

½ teaspoon ground black pepper, divided

3 tablespoons olive oil, divided

1 medium onion, cut into ½-inch dice (about 1 cup)

2 medium carrots, peeled and cut into ¾-inch chunks (about 1 cup)

1 medium celery root (about 10 ounces), peeled and cut into ¾-inch chunks (about 2 cups)

8 ounces red potatoes, cut into ¾-inch chunks (about 1¼ cups)

2 medium white turnips (about 8 ounces), peeled and cut into ¾-inch chunks (about 1¼ cups)

4 garlic cloves, minced

1½ teaspoons chopped fresh thyme or ½ teaspoon dried

3 cups unsalted beef broth

¼ cup all-purpose flour

¼ cup tomato paste

SKILLET
BEEF CHUCK

Good beef stew fills your stomach as it warms your heart. It's as though the long, slow, gentle cooking process imbues us with calm and coaxes us to be tender, just as the heat has done to the meat.

A proper stew can't be rushed. If the heat is too high, it will toughen the meat and prevent the vegetables from sharing their flavors. And you do want them to share: sweet carrots, earthy turnips, refreshing celery root, and starchy potatoes all make valuable contributions to the brothy base.

MAKES 4 SERVINGS

1.  Toss the beef with ½ teaspoon of the salt and ¼ teaspoon of the pepper in a bowl. Heat 2 tablespoons of the oil in a large skillet over medium-high heat. Add half of the beef to the skillet and cook, turning once, until browned, about 4 minutes. Transfer to a plate and repeat with the remaining beef. Set the beef aside.

2.  Reduce the heat to medium and add the remaining 1 tablespoon oil to the skillet. Add the onion, carrots, celery root, potatoes, turnips, garlic, thyme, and the remaining ¼ teaspoon salt and ¼ teaspoon pepper. Cook, stirring occasionally, until the vegetables are slightly softened, 5 to 6 minutes.

3.  Whisk the broth, flour, and tomato paste in a bowl. Add to the skillet with the reserved beef and any juices that have accumulated on the plate. Increase the heat to medium-high and bring to a boil; immediately reduce the heat to medium-low, cover, and simmer until the beef and vegetables are tender, stirring occasionally, about 1 hour 15 minutes. Serve hot.

### FEED YOUR FREEZER

*As is the case with most stews, this freezes beautifully. It has a hardy constitution and is just as good after it's been frozen, heated, cooled, and reheated as it is on the day you first make it. And yes, it can even be reheated in the microwave.*

# FLANK STEAK FAJITAS

2 tablespoons lower-sodium soy sauce

2 tablespoons olive oil

1 teaspoon ground cumin

1 teaspoon garlic powder

1 tablespoon fresh lime juice

1½ pounds flank steak, trimmed

4 bell peppers, assorted colors, cut into ¼-inch-wide strips (about 4 cups)

1 medium red onion, thinly sliced (about 1 cup)

3 plum tomatoes (about 12 ounces), quartered lengthwise

¼ teaspoon salt

### MANGO-CABBAGE SLAW

1 medium mango, peeled and cut into thin strips (about 1¼ cups)

3 cups thinly shredded cabbage

1 jalapeño pepper, seeded and finely chopped

1 tablespoon chopped fresh cilantro

1 tablespoon fresh lime juice

1 tablespoon sugar

¼ teaspoon salt

8 (8-inch) flour tortillas

Sour cream (optional)

SHEET PAN
FLANK STEAK

Besides the fact that they are delicious and satisfying, fajitas have something else going for them: they are fun to build and eat. We usually serve all the ingredients on separate plates and bowls at the table and let everyone build their own. It is a convivial way to eat that we believe promotes sharing good conversation as much as good food.

**MAKES 4 SERVINGS**

1. Preheat the oven to 425°F. Coat a large sheet pan with cooking spray.

2. Combine the soy sauce, oil, cumin, garlic powder, and lime juice in a large bowl. Set aside 2 tablespoons of the mixture. Add the flank steak to the bowl, toss to coat the steak, and let it stand at room temperature for about 20 minutes while you prepare the other ingredients. (Alternatively, the meat may marinate in the refrigerator for up to 12 hours.)

3. Combine the bell peppers, onion, tomatoes, and the reserved 2 tablespoons soy sauce mixture in a bowl; toss well and arrange in a single layer on the sheet pan. Roast the vegetables until they are tender and lightly browned, stirring occasionally, about 20 minutes.

4. Meanwhile, make the mango-cabbage slaw: Combine the mango, cabbage, jalapeño, cilantro, lime juice, sugar, and salt in a bowl; toss well and set aside.

5. Remove the pan from the oven and increase the temperature to 500°F. Slide the vegetables over to one side of the pan. Remove the flank steak from the marinade, letting the excess liquid drip into the bowl. Place the meat on the sheet pan and season it with the salt. Roast the steak, turning once, until an instant-read thermometer inserted horizontally into the thickest part of the meat registers 130°F for medium-rare, 8 to 10 minutes. Transfer the steak to a cutting board and let it rest, loosely covered with foil, about 5 minutes.

6. Warm the tortillas (see opposite). Cut the steak across the grain into thin strips and serve with the tortillas, roasted vegetables, mango-cabbage slaw, and sour cream (if using).

## THREE WAYS TO HEAT TORTILLAS

Heating tortillas makes them more pliable and helps bring out their flavor.

- On the stove: Our favorite method, which imparts a pleasant charred flavor, only works if you have a gas stove. Set the tortilla down directly on the burner over a medium flame until markings appear on the underside. Use tongs to flip the tortilla over briefly. Place the tortillas in a stack on a plate, draping them with a cloth until you are ready to use them.

- In the microwave: If you don't have gas burners, stack the tortillas on a plate, drape with a damp cloth or paper towel, and microwave until they are just warmed through.

- In the oven: Wrap the tortillas in foil and place in a hot oven until they are just heated through (4 to 5 minutes).

# GOCHUJANG SKIRT STEAK

## SCALLION POLENTA + BROCCOLI

3 tablespoons gochujang paste

2 tablespoons honey

1 tablespoon seasoned rice vinegar

1 tablespoon grated fresh ginger

3 garlic cloves, grated on a Microplane

2 tablespoons lower-sodium soy sauce, divided

4 teaspoons toasted sesame oil, divided

1½ pounds skirt steak, trimmed

6 cups broccoli florets (about 1¼ pounds)

1 tablespoon canola oil

¼ teaspoon salt

⅛ teaspoon ground black pepper

1 (18-ounce) tube precooked polenta, cut across into 8 slices

2 scallions, cut diagonally into thin strips (about ⅓ cup)

SHEET PAN
STEAK

You might know gochujang as the fire engine–red sauce served at Korean restaurants. The paste, made from chiles, sticky rice, fermented soybeans, and plenty of salt, has gone from relative obscurity to being a presence on grocery store shelves nearly overnight. Its aggressive, earthy, and slightly sweet flavor is especially good with red meat.

The combination of polenta and Korean-flavored steak might seem odd, but it works quite well. Sweet, nutty polenta slices topped with scallions and soy sauce are a natural with the chewy, juicy steak. We cook the steak on a wire rack above the polenta and broccoli; as it cooks, the juices drip onto the polenta, which happily absorbs it.

**MAKES 4 SERVINGS**

1. Combine the gochujang paste, honey, vinegar, ginger, garlic, 1 tablespoon of the soy sauce, and 2 teaspoons of the sesame oil in a large bowl. Add the skirt steak and turn to completely coat it in the marinade. Let it stand at room temperature for up to 30 minutes, or refrigerate it for up to 2 hours.

2. Preheat the oven to 450°F. Coat a sheet pan with cooking spray.

3. Combine the broccoli, canola oil, salt, and pepper in a bowl. Place the broccoli on the sheet pan in a single uncrowded layer and roast until it just begins to get tender, about 10 minutes.

4. Brush the polenta slices with the remaining 2 teaspoons sesame oil. Slide the broccoli to one side of the pan and set the polenta disks in a single layer on the cleared space. Place a wire rack over the broccoli and polenta.

5. Remove the steak from the bowl and use your fingers to wipe off the excess marinade. Set the steak on the rack and roast until an instant-read thermometer inserted into the thickest part of the steak registers 130°F for medium-rare, 10 to 11 minutes. Let the steak rest for 5 minutes and cut it into ¼-inch-thick slices. Toss the scallions with the remaining 1 tablespoon soy sauce and spoon over the polenta.

# HANGER STEAK AGRODOLCE

## PAN-ROASTED CAULIFLOWER

### AGRODOLCE

1 tablespoon olive oil

2 medium onions, thinly sliced (about 2 cups)

2 tablespoons balsamic vinegar

2 tablespoons sugar

¼ cup golden raisins

1 tablespoon drained nonpareil capers

¼ teaspoon salt

⅛ teaspoon ground black pepper

2 plum tomatoes (8 ounces), seeded and diced (about 1 cup)

1½ pounds hanger steak

¾ teaspoon salt, divided

¼ teaspoon ground black pepper

3 tablespoons olive oil, divided

6 cups cauliflower florets (from 1 small head; about 1½ pounds)

### SKILLET
### STEAK

Hanger steak is also known by its very telling nickname: the butcher's steak. The hanger was not considered an attractive-looking piece of meat, so butchers—who appreciated what an incredibly flavorful, juicy cut it is—would set it aside to take home for themselves.

Hanger is a relatively inexpensive, tender cut (a rare thing when it comes to the most flavorful steaks). It is perfectly delicious when seasoned with nothing more than salt and pepper, but agrodolce sauce takes it to a whole new level.

Agrodolce is an Italian sweet and sour sauce made with vinegar and sugar—and a whole lot of other ingredients at the cook's discretion. Our version starts with caramelized onions, to which we add a sprinkling of golden raisins and capers and the surprise of diced tomato. The sauce is wonderful on steak-like fish (we're looking at you, tuna) as well as chicken and pork. It is also delightful draped over a creamy, ripe Brie.

**MAKES 4 SERVINGS**

1. Preheat the oven to 400°F.
2. Make the agrodolce: Heat the oil in a large skillet over medium heat. Add the onions and cook, stirring occasionally, until they are softened and golden, 10 to 12 minutes. Add the vinegar, sugar, raisins, capers, salt, and pepper and simmer until the liquid is thick and syrupy, 2 to 3 minutes. Stir in the tomatoes and cook 2 minutes longer or until they are softened; transfer to a bowl.
3. Season the steak with ½ teaspoon of the salt and the pepper. Heat 1 tablespoon of the oil in the skillet over medium-high heat. Add the steak and cook until browned, turning once, about 6 minutes (it will not be fully cooked). Transfer the steak to a plate.
4. Reduce the heat to medium and add the remaining 2 tablespoons oil to the skillet. Add the cauliflower and the remaining ¼ teaspoon salt; cook, stirring occasionally, until it is lightly browned, 6 to 7 minutes. Remove from the heat.

5. Slide the cauliflower to the sides of the skillet and add the steak in the center. Transfer to the oven and roast until an instant-read thermometer inserted horizontally into the thickest part of the steak registers 130°F for medium-rare and the cauliflower is crisp-tender, 9 to 10 minutes.

6. Transfer the steak to a cutting board and let it rest 5 minutes before cutting it across into ½-inch-thick slices. Serve it topped with the agrodolce and accompanied by the cauliflower.

# SPANISH CHUCK EYE STEAK

12 ounces green beans, trimmed

2 tablespoons unsalted butter, cut into small pieces

¾ teaspoon salt, divided

¼ teaspoon plus ⅛ teaspoon ground black pepper, divided

4 (6- to 7-ounce) boneless chuck eye steaks

½ teaspoon dried oregano

2 tablespoons olive oil, divided

1 medium onion, thinly sliced (about 1 cup)

3 garlic cloves, sliced

2 teaspoons sugar

1 (7.5-ounce) jar roasted red peppers, drained and thinly sliced

16 small pimiento-stuffed olives, halved across

1 tablespoon sherry vinegar

2 (10-ounce) bags frozen cooked white rice

3 tablespoons sliced natural almonds

2 tablespoons chopped fresh parsley

SKILLET
STEAK

A little known, inexpensive, and very flavorful cut of meat called chuck eye (see opposite) is topped with meltingly soft onions, roasted peppers, green olives, and a splash of sherry vinegar. The entire meal, including green beans and almond-parsley rice, is on the table in about 30 minutes.

**MAKES 4 SERVINGS**

1. Preheat the oven to 450°F.
2. Combine the green beans, butter, ¼ teaspoon of the salt, and ⅛ teaspoon of the pepper in a bowl. Arrange the beans in a single layer on half of a 24-inch length of foil, fold the foil over, and crimp the edges. Place the packet on the oven rack to one side and steam-roast until the beans are crisp-tender, about 20 minutes.
3. Meanwhile, season the steaks with the oregano, ¼ teaspoon of the salt, and the remaining ¼ teaspoon pepper.
4. Heat 1 tablespoon of the oil in a large ovenproof skillet over medium-high heat. Add the onion, garlic, and sugar and cook, stirring occasionally, until the onion is slightly softened, 3 to 4 minutes. Stir in the roasted peppers, olives, vinegar, and remaining ¼ teaspoon salt; cook until the onion is completely soft, 1 to 2 minutes. Transfer the topping to a bowl. Wipe out the skillet with a paper towel.
5. Heat the remaining 1 tablespoon oil in the skillet over medium-high heat. Add the steaks and cook, turning once, until they are browned, about 6 minutes. Place the skillet in the oven and roast until an instant-read thermometer inserted horizontally into the thickest part of the steak registers 130°F for medium-rare, 3 to 4 minutes. Transfer the steaks to a cutting board, tent loosely with foil, and let them rest for 3 to 5 minutes.
6. Return the topping to the skillet and reheat over medium-high for 1 minute. Remove the green beans packet from the oven.
7. Microwave the rice according to package directions; transfer to a serving bowl and stir in the almonds and parsley.
8. Spoon the topping over the steaks and serve with the rice and green beans.

## STEAK SECRETS

Chuck eye is the cut of meat nobody talks about. It is as flavorful as a rib eye but far less expensive and a little chewier. (Then again, rib eye is hardly a tender cut! It is lauded for its great flavor, not its tenderness.)

Don't confuse "chuck eye" with "chuck steak." Chuck *eyes* are cut one rib down from the rib eye, and there are only two available per cow, which means they are not as readily available. However, if you ask in advance at the meat counter at your grocery store, chances are good that if they don't have it, they can easily get it. (We've had great luck at Whole Foods.)

Take care when cooking a chuck eye to not overdo it: at medium-rare, it will be at its most tender—and will be remarkably flavorful. Insert an instant-read meat thermometer horizontally until the tip is at least 1 inch deep in the center of the thickest part of the steak; it should register 130°F.

# LONDON BROIL WITH DIJON-BALSAMIC VINAIGRETTE

1 teaspoon ground coriander

½ teaspoon onion powder

1 teaspoon salt, divided

½ teaspoon ground black pepper, divided

1½ pounds top round London broil

1 pound small red potatoes, quartered

1 teaspoon chopped fresh rosemary

2 tablespoons olive oil, divided

2 medium zucchini (about 1 pound), halved lengthwise and cut across into ½-inch-thick slices

### DIJON-BALSAMIC VINAIGRETTE

1 tablespoon balsamic vinegar

1 tablespoon chopped shallots

2 teaspoons Dijon mustard

¼ teaspoon salt

3 tablespoons extra virgin olive oil

### SHEET PAN
LONDON BROIL

This is a riff on another one of David's childhood favorites. His mother, like so many of her time, marinated London broil in bottled Italian dressing. David adds depth by patting the surface with spices to intensify the flavor while it cooks. We drizzle the cooked, sliced steak with a vinaigrette just before serving.

Here's a sort of crazy thing: although we think of London broil as a cut of meat (and it may be labeled in the meat case as such), the name technically refers to a preparation method (marinating, broiling or grilling, and thinly slicing). It is often made with top round, a relatively inexpensive cut that is lean and flavorful. But it is not tender, which is why it is important to serve it very thinly sliced across the grain.

As with other lean cuts, the meat will be at its most tender when cooked to medium-rare. If you have one family member who wants it well-done, serve them the end pieces.

**MAKES 4 SERVINGS**

1. Preheat the oven to 450°F. Coat a sheet pan with cooking spray.
2. Combine the coriander, onion powder, ½ teaspoon of the salt, and ¼ teaspoon of the pepper in a small bowl. Rub the mixture over the London broil and let stand at room temperature for 15 minutes.
3. Combine the potatoes, rosemary, and 1 tablespoon of the oil in a bowl. Toss with ¼ teaspoon of the salt and ⅛ teaspoon of the pepper. Arrange on the sheet pan in a single layer and roast for 15 minutes.
4. Meanwhile, combine the zucchini with the remaining 1 tablespoon oil. Toss with the remaining ¼ teaspoon salt and ⅛ teaspoon pepper.
5. Remove the sheet pan from the oven and slide the potatoes to one side of the pan. Add the zucchini to the cleared space in a single layer and top with a wire rack. Place the meat on the wire rack.

6. Position an oven rack 4 to 5 inches below the heat source and preheat the broiler.

7. Broil the steak and vegetables, turning the steak once, until an instant-read thermometer inserted into the thickest part of the steak registers 130°F for medium-rare, 8 to 10 minutes. Transfer the meat to a cutting board and let it rest 5 minutes; slice it thinly across the grain.

8. While the meat rests, make the vinaigrette: Combine the vinegar, shallots, mustard, and salt in a bowl. Slowly whisk in the oil. Just before serving, drizzle the steak with the dressing.

## ACROSS THE GRAIN

With London broil, when you cut *across the grain* you will go from one long side to the other. (That doesn't hold true with every cut of meat, it just depends on the shape of a particular cut.) If you can't tell where the grain is on the top side, flip it over: chances are it will be easier for you to spot on the underside. (That *is* the case with every cut of meat.)

LONDON BROIL WITH DIJON-BALSAMIC VINAIGRETTE 110

# RIB EYE STEAKS WITH THYME-SHALLOT BUTTER

**PAPRIKA POTATOES + ASPARAGUS**

3 tablespoons unsalted butter, softened

1 tablespoon finely chopped shallot

1 teaspoon chopped fresh thyme

1 teaspoon grated lemon zest

1¼ teaspoons salt, divided

1 pound small red potatoes, quartered lengthwise

2 tablespoons olive oil, divided

1 teaspoon sweet paprika

½ teaspoon ground black pepper, divided

1 pound asparagus, trimmed

2 (1-pound) bone-in rib eye steaks, about 1 inch thick

SHEET PAN
STEAK

We think of rib eye steaks as a special-occasion meal; they are costly and far from lean—but, boy, are they good! This is a meal we might make to celebrate with friends, or just with each other; or on a Friday night to mark the end of a particularly crazy week.

Buy rib eyes that are about 1 inch thick. Any thicker than that and the outside might get overdone before the center is medium-rare.

The herbed butter takes these steaks to an even more decadent level, but this classic steak-and-potatoes meal is also wonderful without it. You can, of course, make extra herbed butter and keep it in the refrigerator or freezer to use on potatoes, rice, corn, or anything and everything else on which butter gets slathered.

MAKES 4 SERVINGS

1. Preheat the oven to 425°F. Coat a sheet pan with cooking spray.

2. Use a fork to mash the butter with the shallot, thyme, lemon zest, and ¼ teaspoon of the salt in a small bowl. Transfer it to the center of a small sheet of plastic wrap and roll it into a 1-inch-diameter log; twist the ends closed and chill in the freezer to harden until ready to use.

3. Combine the potatoes with 1 tablespoon of the oil in a bowl. Toss with the paprika, ¼ teaspoon of the salt and ⅛ teaspoon of the pepper. Arrange the potatoes in a single layer around the edges of the sheet pan. Roast for 20 minutes, rotating the pan front to back after 10 minutes.

4. Meanwhile, combine the asparagus with the remaining 1 tablespoon oil. Toss with the remaining ¼ teaspoon of the salt and ⅛ teaspoon of the pepper.

5. After the potatoes have roasted 20 minutes, add the asparagus to the center of the sheet pan. Roast for 10 minutes, until the vegetables are tender. Transfer the potatoes and asparagus to a serving platter and tent with foil to keep warm.

6. Position an oven rack 4 to 5 inches below the heat source and preheat the broiler.

7. Season the steaks with the remaining ½ teaspoon salt and ¼ teaspoon pepper and place them on the sheet pan. Broil, turning them once, until an instant-read thermometer inserted horizontally into the thickest part of the steak registers 130°F for medium-rare, 6 to 8 minutes. Serve the steaks topped with a slice of the butter.

# BEEF TENDERLOIN STEAKS WITH MUSHROOM-RED WINE REDUCTION

**BROCCOLINI + COUSCOUS**

1¼ teaspoons salt, divided

1 cup couscous

3 tablespoons olive oil, divided

4 garlic cloves, thinly sliced

1 pound broccolini, trimmed

½ teaspoon ground black pepper, divided

4 ounces white mushrooms, quartered

4 (5- to 6-ounce) beef tenderloin steaks, 1½ inches thick

1 medium shallot, finely chopped (about ¼ cup)

½ teaspoon chopped fresh thyme or ⅛ teaspoon dried

½ cup dry red wine, such as Cabernet Sauvignon

¾ cup unsalted chicken broth

1 tablespoon unsalted butter

SKILLET
STEAKS

Beef tenderloin is one of the most tender cuts of beef, which makes it easy to eat and more forgiving if it is a little overcooked. The trade-off for that tenderness is that it is milder tasting than most other steaks. That's why we usually pair it with foods that amp up its beefy flavor—like the mushrooms in this savory sauce.

This is an elegant meal: graceful broccolini, nutty couscous, and juicy seared steaks are as well suited for a special occasion as for a simple weeknight.

**MAKES 4 SERVINGS**

1. Preheat the oven to 200°F.
2. Combine 1¼ cups water and ¼ teaspoon of the salt in a medium microwave-safe bowl. Microwave on high until the water just starts to boil, 3 to 4 minutes. Remove from the microwave, stir in the couscous, cover with plastic wrap and let it stand. (The couscous will absorb the liquid.)
3. Heat 1 tablespoon of the oil in a large skillet over medium heat. Add the garlic and cook until it just begins to brown, 1 to 1½ minutes. Add the broccolini and cook, tossing, for 1 minute. Add ½ cup water, cover the skillet, and cook until the broccolini is bright green and crisp-tender, 2 to 3 minutes. Uncover the skillet and cook until the water evaporates, about 1 minute more; season with ¼ teaspoon of the salt and ⅛ teaspoon of the pepper. Transfer to a plate and keep the broccolini warm in the oven.
4. Return the skillet to the stove and heat 1 tablespoon of the oil over medium heat. Add the mushrooms and ⅛ teaspoon of the salt and cook, stirring occasionally, until lightly browned, about 4 minutes. Transfer to a bowl and set aside.
5. Season the steaks with ½ teaspoon of the salt and ¼ teaspoon of the pepper. Heat the remaining 1 tablespoon oil in the skillet over medium heat. Add the steaks and cook, turning once, until they are browned and an instant-read thermometer inserted into the thickest

## BROCCOLINI

*Broccolini has slender stems and flowering buds similar to, but more delicate than, broccoli florets. It is not baby broccoli but a hybrid—a cross between broccoli and Chinese broccoli or gai lan, which is more similar to kale than to broccoli.*

*Unlike broccoli, the stalks are as appealing to eat as the florets. Broccolini is milder and sweeter than broccoli, with none of the bitterness of broccoli rabe.*

part of the steak registers 130°F for medium-rare, 9 to 10 minutes. Transfer the steaks to a plate and tent loosely with foil.

6. Add the shallot and thyme to the skillet and cook over medium heat, stirring, for 30 seconds. Add the wine, bring to a boil, and cook for 2 minutes to slightly reduce the liquid. Increase the heat to medium-high, add the broth, and bring to a boil. Cook until the liquid is slightly thickened, about 4 minutes. Add the mushrooms and continue cooking until the sauce is just thick enough to coat the back of a spoon, 2 to 3 minutes. Remove the skillet from the heat and stir in the butter and the remaining ⅛ teaspoon salt and ⅛ teaspoon pepper; stir until the butter is melted. Spoon over the steaks and serve with the broccolini and couscous.

# MA PO TOFU

1 (16-ounce) package firm tofu, drained

½ cup unsalted chicken broth

2 tablespoons lower-sodium soy sauce

1 tablespoon oyster-flavored sauce

1 tablespoon chili-garlic sauce

1 tablespoon cornstarch

1 tablespoon canola oil

8 ounces sliced button mushrooms

¼ teaspoon salt

8 ounces lean ground pork

4 garlic cloves, minced

1 tablespoon minced fresh ginger

1 teaspoon toasted sesame oil

3 scallions, chopped (about ⅓ cup)

2 (10-ounce) bags cooked frozen white rice

SKILLET
GROUND PORK

The story goes that this fiery dish of crumbled pork and tofu got its name from the woman in the Qing dynasty who used to pass the dish out to workers. Ma po translates as "pockmarked old woman"; her face was covered with smallpox scars. Looking at the dish, we can't help but wonder if it is named for the little pocks of spicy crumbled pork clinging to the silken squares of tofu.

Traditionally, the dish is made with mouth-numbing Sichuan peppercorns; we've substituted Asian chili-garlic paste, which is sold in grocery stores. (It won't numb your mouth, but it does pack a powerful fiery punch.) The dish has some but not a lot of heat, turn it up or down by adding more or less of the chili sauce.

**MAKES 4 SERVINGS**

1. Press the tofu: Place the tofu on a dinner plate, set a second plate on top of it, and let it stand 15 to 20 minutes. Discard the liquid that accumulates on the plate and cut the tofu into ½-inch cubes.

2. Combine the chicken broth, soy sauce, oyster-flavored sauce, chili-garlic sauce, and cornstarch in a bowl and stir until the cornstarch is dissolved.

3. Heat the canola oil in a large skillet over medium-high heat. Add the mushrooms and salt and cook, stirring occasionally, until lightly browned, 5 to 6 minutes. Transfer the mushrooms to a bowl.

4. Return the skillet to medium-high heat and add the pork; cook, breaking it into smaller pieces with a wooden spoon, until it is no longer pink, 3 to 4 minutes. Add the garlic and ginger and cook until fragrant, 30 to 45 seconds. Stir in the tofu and cook until it starts to brown, about 4 minutes. Add the reserved mushrooms, broth mixture, and sesame oil; bring to a boil and cook, stirring, until thickened, about 1 minute. Remove from the heat and stir in the scallions.

5. Microwave the rice according to package directions and serve with the tofu.

# SHAVED VEGETABLE AND PROSCIUTTO PIZZA

1 pound pizza dough, homemade (recipe follows) or store-bought

6 ounces part-skim mozzarella cheese, shredded

1 cup part-skim ricotta cheese

1 medium zucchini (about 8 ounces), trimmed and shaved with a vegetable peeler

4 white mushrooms, thinly sliced

1 tablespoon extra virgin olive oil

⅓ cup grated Pecorino Romano cheese

2 ounces thinly sliced prosciutto, torn into bite-size pieces

½ cup oil-packed sun-dried tomatoes, drained and thinly sliced

SHEET PAN
PIZZA

Thin ribbons of zucchini, slivers of sun-dried tomato, wisps of prosciutto, and slender meaty mushrooms nestle together on a bed of creamy ricotta and mozzarella to top this pizza crust.

You can make your own dough (see opposite) or buy it ready-made from your local pizzeria or the grocery store. Whatever way you go, be sure you have an extra to keep in the freezer. You never know when a pizza emergency will arise.

MAKES 4 SERVINGS

1. Preheat the oven to 500°F. Coat a sheet pan with cooking spray.
2. Place the dough on the sheet pan and stretch to fit. (Work from the center outward so you don't get skinny, torn edges and a thick crust in the middle.)
3. Combine the mozzarella and ricotta in a bowl. Spread the top of the dough with the ricotta mixture, leaving a ½-inch border around the edge. Toss the zucchini and mushrooms with the oil and arrange over the cheese in an even layer. Sprinkle the Romano over the top.
4. Bake the pizza until the edges of the dough are lightly browned and the vegetables are tender, 14 to 15 minutes. Top with the prosciutto and sun-dried tomatoes. Bake until heated through, about 2 minutes longer. Remove from the oven and let it rest 3 minutes or so before slicing.

# DAVID'S NO-FAIL HOMEMADE PIZZA DOUGH

We always make an extra batch of this to feed the freezer. It keeps well for several months (if you somehow haven't used it by then) when wrapped tightly in plastic wrap and slid into a heavy-duty, freezer-worthy plastic zip-top bag.

¾ cup plus 2 tablespoons warm water (100° to 110°F)

1 (0.75-ounce) packet active dry yeast

2 teaspoons sugar

1 tablespoon plus 2 teaspoons extra virgin olive oil, divided

2 cups all-purpose flour, plus extra for dusting the work surface

¼ cup cornmeal (fine to medium grind)

½ teaspoon salt

1. Combine the water, yeast, sugar, and 1 tablespoon of the oil in a small bowl; let stand 5 minutes or until the mixture is bubbly.
2. Combine the flour, cornmeal, and salt in a large bowl and stir in the yeast mixture until a rough dough forms. Knead the dough with your hands in the bowl once or twice or until it comes together. Turn the dough out onto a lightly floured surface and knead it with the heels of your hands until smooth and elastic, 5 to 7 minutes. Place the dough in a large bowl and drizzle it with the remaining 2 teaspoons oil, turning to coat.
3. Cover the bowl with plastic wrap and let the dough rise in a warm place (85° to 100°F) for 1 hour or until doubled in size. (Press two fingers into the dough. If an indentation remains, the dough has risen enough.) Press down on the dough to deflate it and let it rest for 5 minutes.

# PORK CHOPS WITH PAN-ROASTED GRAPE RELISH

BRUSSELS SPROUTS + FINGERLING POTATOES

2 tablespoons plus 1 teaspoon olive oil, divided

12 ounces Brussels sprouts, trimmed and quartered lengthwise

12 ounces fingerling potatoes, quartered lengthwise

1 teaspoon salt, divided

½ teaspoon ground black pepper, divided

4 (5- to 6-ounce) boneless center-cut pork chops

2 cups seedless red and green grapes, halved

1 small shallot, finely chopped (about 3 tablespoons)

¼ teaspoon dried thyme

¼ cup dry sherry wine

1 tablespoon balsamic vinegar

1 tablespoon sugar

1 tablespoon unsalted butter

SKILLET
PORK CHOPS

Grapes make the basis for this unusual and very pretty relish. Looks only go so far, of course: beneath its charming appearance, the relish has a wonderful nuanced flavor thanks to a careful balance of acid (from the balsamic and sherry) and sweet (from the grapes).

**MAKES 4 SERVINGS**

1. Preheat the oven to 425°F. Brush the bottom of a large ovenproof skillet with 1 teaspoon of the oil.

2. Combine the Brussels sprouts, fingerlings, and 1 tablespoon of the oil in a bowl. Toss with ¼ teaspoon of the salt and ¼ teaspoon of the pepper. Transfer to the skillet and roast in the oven, stirring occasionally, until the potatoes are tender and the Brussels sprouts have browned, 26 to 28 minutes. Transfer the vegetables to a bowl and drape loosely with foil to keep warm.

3. Season the pork chops with ½ teaspoon of the salt and the remaining ¼ teaspoon pepper. Heat the remaining 1 tablespoon oil in the skillet over medium-high heat, add the pork, and cook, turning once, until lightly browned, about 4 minutes. (The pork will not be cooked through.) Transfer the chops to a plate and set aside.

4. Add the grapes to the skillet and cook, stirring occasionally, until they begin to burst, 2 to 3 minutes. Add the shallot and thyme and cook until fragrant, about 1 minute. Stir in the sherry, balsamic, sugar, and remaining ¼ teaspoon salt; bring to a boil and cook until the liquid starts to thicken, about 2 minutes. Move the grapes to the sides of the skillet and add the pork chops; cook, turning once or twice, until a thermometer inserted horizontally into the center of the chops registers 140°F, 2 to 3 minutes. Transfer to a plate.

5. Swirl the butter into the skillet with the grape mixture until it is melted. Serve the sauce spooned over the pork chops.

## IS IT DONE YET?

I didn't grow up eating pork for dinner (my family is Jewish, but we ate bacon); for David, it was a staple. While I certainly learned to cook and appreciate it in culinary school, it wasn't until I met David that I really incorporated it into my rotation of regular family dinners. I think it was because, despite my training, I tended to overcook it.

There is no trichinosis in this country anymore (that used to be the big health concern with pork), and even the USDA has lowered the recommended temperature to which pork needs to be cooked to 145°F (from 160°F). The truth is, pork is raised much leaner now and really should—and can safely—be served with some pink in the center. At that point the meat will be moist and tender and still have flavor. We cook pork to 140°F. By the time it gets to the table, it hits about 145°F.

# PORK CHOPS WITH ITALIAN SALSA VERDE

1 pound sweet potatoes, peeled, halved lengthwise, and cut across into ½-inch-thick slices

3 tablespoons olive oil, divided

1 teaspoon salt, divided

Italian Salsa Verde (recipe follows)

1 pound broccoli rabe, trimmed

3 garlic cloves, thinly sliced

⅛ teaspoon crushed red pepper flakes (or to taste)

4 (8-ounce) bone-in pork chops, about ½ inch thick

¼ teaspoon ground black pepper

SHEET PAN
PORK CHOPS

Truth: Italian salsa verde makes everything taste better. (Okay, maybe I wouldn't put it on ice cream . . . but only maybe.) It is simple to make—you just dump everything in the blender—but has layers of flavor, thanks to umami-rich anchovy, bright lemon juice, and briny capers, all against the backdrop of grassy parsley. The sauce brings out the meatiness of pork chops and is the perfect complement to creamy sweet potatoes and the bitter punch of broccoli rabe.

We broil the pork chops on a wire rack to ensure they get lovely crisped edges.

**MAKES 4 SERVINGS**

1. Preheat the oven to 425°F. Coat a sheet pan with cooking spray.

2. Combine the sweet potatoes and 1 tablespoon of the oil in a medium bowl. Toss with ¼ teaspoon of the salt; transfer to the sheet pan and spread into a single layer. Roast for 10 minutes.

3. While the sweet potatoes cook, make the salsa verde. Combine the broccoli rabe with 1 tablespoon of the oil, ¼ teaspoon of the salt, the garlic, and red pepper flakes.

4. When the sweet potatoes have roasted 10 minutes, stir and slide them to one side of the sheet pan. Add the broccoli rabe to the pan and roast until tender, tossing once, about 12 minutes. Transfer to a serving platter and drape loosely with foil to keep warm.

5. Position an oven rack 4 to 5 inches below the heat source and preheat the broiler. Place a wire rack on the sheet pan.

6. Rub the pork chops with the remaining 1 tablespoon oil and season with the remaining ½ teaspoon salt and the pepper. Set them on the wire rack and broil, turning once, until an instant-read thermometer inserted horizontally into the thickest part of the largest chop registers 140°F, 8 to 10 minutes. Serve the salsa verde spooned over the chops.

## ITALIAN SALSA VERDE

1½ cups fresh parsley leaves

1 oil-packed anchovy fillet, drained

1 garlic clove, peeled

3 tablespoons olive oil

1 tablespoon fresh lemon juice

2 teaspoons drained nonpareil capers

¼ teaspoon salt

Combine the parsley, anchovy, garlic, oil, lemon juice, capers, and salt in a blender and puree.

# SMOTHERED PORK CHOPS

⅓ cup all-purpose flour

1 teaspoon sweet paprika

1 teaspoon garlic powder

¾ teaspoon ground cumin

1 teaspoon salt, divided

¾ teaspoon ground black pepper, divided

4 (8-ounce) bone-in pork chops, about ½ inch thick

¾ cup quick-cooking grits

5 slices thick-cut smoked bacon, coarsely chopped

1½ pounds collard greens, center ribs removed, cut into bite-size pieces (about 10 cups)

1½ cups unsalted chicken broth

2 tablespoons unsalted butter

1 tablespoon olive oil

2 large Vidalia or other sweet onions, thinly sliced (about 3 cups)

SKILLET
PORK CHOPS

I'm sure David was a Southern cook in a former life. He may have been a rather rotund one, too, given that he is as passionate about *eating* Southern food as he is about creating it.

I'd happily make a meal out of the collard greens and grits alone. (Okay, truth: I did right after we photographed it.) The very thought of that is anathema to my meat-loving husband. I tried to explain that it's not that I don't like the pork chops, it is about how much I *love* greens and grits, but he just looked at me as if I'd slapped his mother. Then he ate my pork chop.

**MAKES 4 SERVINGS**

1. Preheat the oven to 200°F.

2. Combine the flour, paprika, garlic powder, cumin, ¼ teaspoon of the salt, and ¼ teaspoon of the pepper on a plate. Dredge the pork chops, one at a time, until they are lightly and evenly coated. Measure out 2 tablespoons of the seasoned flour remaining on the plate and set aside.

3. Bring 3 cups water, ¼ teaspoon of the salt, and the remaining ½ teaspoon pepper to a boil in a large skillet over medium-high heat. Whisk in the grits, reduce the heat to medium-low, cover, and simmer until thickened, about 5 minutes. Transfer the grits to an ovenproof serving dish, cover with foil, and keep warm in the oven.

4. Wipe out the skillet with a paper towel and return it to the stove over medium heat. Add the bacon and cook until it is browned and crisp, 6 to 7 minutes. Add the collard greens a few handfuls at a time, adding more as the greens wilt. Cook, stirring occasionally, until they are tender and bright green, 6 to 7 minutes. Season with ¼ teaspoon of the salt. Transfer to a bowl, cover, and keep warm in the oven.

5. Whisk the reserved seasoned flour with the chicken broth until smooth and set aside.

6. Melt the butter with the oil in the skillet over medium heat. Add the pork chops and cook, turning once, until they are browned and *just* cooked through, 8 to 9 minutes. Transfer the chops to a plate.

7. Add the onions to the skillet and cook, stirring occasionally, until tender, 6 to 7 minutes. Give the broth mixture a stir (the flour may have settled to the bottom) and pour it into the skillet; bring to a boil. Stir in the remaining ¼ teaspoon salt and cook until the liquid thickens, about 1 minute. Return the pork chops to the pan and cook, turning once or twice, until they are heated through, about 1 minute. Serve the sauce spooned over the pork chops with the collard greens and grits on the side.

# CHERRY-CHIPOTLE PORK TENDERLOIN

1½ pounds sweet potatoes, peeled and cut into 1-inch chunks

3 tablespoons olive oil, divided

¼ teaspoon ground cinnamon

1 teaspoon salt, divided

¼ teaspoon ground black pepper, divided

12 ounces green beans, trimmed

1 teaspoon grated or thinly sliced lemon zest

1 (1½-pound) pork tenderloin, trimmed

1 teaspoon chili powder

1 teaspoon ground cumin

½ cup cherry preserves

¼ teaspoon chipotle chile powder

SHEET PAN
PORK TENDERLOIN

There is something about the combination of the full fruity flavor of cherries with smoky heat that is particularly compelling—and nearly addictive. (I won't admit to licking the spoon.) They belong together—and are arguably at their very best when paired with pork.

This meal comes together easily: the pork is rubbed with aromatic cumin and chili powder and roasted surrounded by cinnamon-dusted chunks of sweet potato and a foil packet of steam-roasted green beans. With very little prep work, the complete meal is on the table in less than 45 minutes.

MAKES 4 SERVINGS

1. Preheat the oven to 425°F. Coat a sheet pan with cooking spray.
2. Toss the sweet potatoes with 1 tablespoon of the oil in a medium bowl. Toss with the cinnamon, ¼ teaspoon of the salt, and ⅛ teaspoon of the pepper.
3. Combine the green beans and 1 tablespoon of the oil in a medium bowl. Toss with the lemon zest, ¼ teaspoon of the salt, and the remaining ⅛ teaspoon pepper. Arrange the beans in a single layer on one half of a 24-inch length of foil and fold the foil over, crimping the edges to form a packet.
4. Rub the pork all over with the remaining 1 tablespoon olive oil. Mix the chili powder, cumin, and remaining ½ teaspoon salt in a small bowl. Pat the mixture over the entire surface of the pork and place it in the center of the sheet pan. Arrange the sweet potato chunks around the pork in a single layer. Roast for 5 minutes; add the green bean packet to the oven on the rack below the sheet pan. Roast for 15 minutes.
5. Combine the preserves and chipotle powder and brush half of it over the pork. Toss the sweet potatoes and roast for 10 minutes. Brush the pork with the remaining glaze and continue cooking until an instant-read thermometer inserted into the thickest part of the pork registers 140°F, about 3 minutes more. Let the pork rest 5 minutes before slicing.

# ROSEMARY ROAST PORK TENDERLOIN

1 (1½-pound) butternut squash, peeled and halved lengthwise

2 medium red onions, cut through the root end into 6 wedges each

6 dried Mission figs, halved

3 tablespoons olive oil, divided

3 tablespoons balsamic vinegar

1 tablespoon lightly packed light brown sugar

½ teaspoon salt

¼ teaspoon ground black pepper

### ROSEMARY RUB

2 teaspoons finely chopped fresh rosemary or ½ teaspoon ground dried rosemary

1 teaspoon garlic powder

½ teaspoon ground coriander

½ teaspoon salt

¼ teaspoon ground black pepper

1 (1½-pound) pork tenderloin, trimmed

1 (5-ounce) package baby spinach (about 6 cups)

### SHEET PAN
PORK TENDERLOIN

This is one of those rare sheet-pan dinners in which almost all the elements go on the pan together and cook for the same amount of time. That makes it perfect for when the day has sucked out every last bit of your brain juice and all you want to do is Sit. Down.

If you aren't up to dealing with a butternut squash, buy it already peeled and cut up; most grocery stores sell it in the produce section in ready-to-cook chunks. You will need about 3 cups for this recipe. (If the chunks are bigger than 1 inch, cut them in half so they cook through by the time the pork is ready.)

The pork may be seasoned with fresh or dried rosemary. If you use dried, be sure to get dried *ground* rosemary—the dried *leaves* are like sharp little twigs in your mouth.

We love the figs in this—for both the earthy sweetness and the crunch of the seeds, which adds textural contrast. The spinach, which wilts in the pan while the pork rests, adds a fresh, green note and more vegetables to help round out the meal.

**MAKES 4 SERVINGS**

1. Preheat the oven to 450°F. Coat a sheet pan with cooking spray.
2. Cut the squash across into ½-inch-thick slices. Combine them in a large bowl with the onion wedges, figs, and 2 tablespoons of the oil. Toss thoroughly; add the vinegar, brown sugar, salt, and pepper and toss again. Arrange in a single layer on the sheet pan.
3. Make the rub: Combine the rosemary, garlic powder, coriander, salt, and pepper in a small bowl.
4. Place the pork on a work surface and rub it with the remaining 1 tablespoon oil. Pat the rosemary mixture over the entire surface of the pork.
5. Place the pork in the center of the sheet pan and roast until the vegetables are very tender and an instant-read thermometer inserted

## THINKING AHEAD

*Plan ahead for an additional meal. Add a second pork tenderloin to the pan; you can use it in place of the chicken for the Bánh Mì (page 20), add it to the Ooey Gooey Mac and Cheese (page 223), or stir it into the Baked Risotto with Shiitakes and Asparagus (page 248).*

into the thickest part of the pork registers 140°F, 25 to 27 minutes. Remove from the oven and transfer the pork to a cutting board. Tent loosely with foil and let rest 5 minutes.

6. Stir the spinach into the vegetables on the sheet pan and return to the oven. Roast the vegetables until the spinach starts to wilt, about 3 minutes.

7. Cut the pork across into slices and serve with the vegetables.

# ROAST PORK LOIN WITH ARUGULA-PARSLEY PESTO

POTATO-FENNEL HASH

## ARUGULA-PARSLEY PESTO

3 tablespoons blanched almonds

2 cups baby arugula

1 cup fresh parsley leaves

1 garlic clove

¼ cup grated Pecorino Romano cheese

½ cup olive oil

¼ teaspoon salt

2 teaspoons dried oregano

1 teaspoon dried basil

1 teaspoon garlic powder

¾ teaspoon ground cumin

¾ teaspoon salt, divided

½ teaspoon ground black pepper, divided

2 pounds center-cut pork loin, trimmed

1 large fennel bulb (about 1 pound), trimmed and cut into ½-inch-thick slices

1 pound baby potatoes, halved

1 large red onion, chopped (about 1½ cups)

1 tablespoon olive oil

## SHEET PAN
## PORK LOIN

While the ingredient list looks long, this is a very simple meal to put together. After you toast the nuts for the pesto, you simply combine the seasoning for the pork and rub it over the surface. The hash, which we love rewarmed the next day, is a matter of simply cutting up three vegetables. It all goes in the oven together, gets one stir during cooking, and you're done.

Arugula gives the pesto a little edgy bite; enough to make us want to use it as a sandwich spread, a vegetable dip, or topping for fish.

**MAKES 4 SERVINGS**

1. Preheat the oven to 350°F.
2. Arrange the almonds on a sheet pan and bake until they are lightly toasted, 5 to 6 minutes; transfer to a bowl and set aside for the pesto.
3. Coat the sheet pan with cooking spray.
4. Prepare the pork and hash: Combine the oregano, basil, garlic powder, cumin, ½ teaspoon of the salt, and ¼ teaspoon of the pepper in a small bowl. Pat the mixture evenly over the entire surface of the pork and place the pork on the sheet pan.
5. Combine the fennel, potatoes, onion, and oil in a bowl. Toss with the remaining ¼ teaspoon salt and ¼ teaspoon pepper; arrange the vegetables around the pork.
6. Roast for 30 minutes; stir the vegetables and continue roasting until the vegetables are tender and an instant-read thermometer inserted into the thickest part of the pork registers 140°F, 18 to 20 minutes more. Let the pork rest 5 minutes before slicing.
7. While the pork is in the oven, make the arugula-parsley pesto: Combine the cooled almonds, arugula, parsley, garlic, Romano, oil, and salt in a blender; puree.
8. Spoon the pesto over the pork and serve with the fennel and potatoes.

# APRICOT-HONEY SPARE RIBS

SMASH-ROASTED POTATOES + GREEN SALAD WITH PARSLEY VINAIGRETTE

2 tablespoons lightly packed dark brown sugar

1 teaspoon garlic powder

1 teaspoon smoked paprika

1 teaspoon chili powder

¼ teaspoon ground ginger

1¼ teaspoons salt, divided

16 sliced bone-in pork spare ribs (4½ to 5 pounds)

12 small red potatoes (about 1 pound), halved

1 tablespoon olive oil

¼ teaspoon ground black pepper

⅔ cup apricot preserves

2 tablespoons honey

1 tablespoon cider vinegar

SHEET PAN
PORK SPARE RIBS

David's mother used to make ribs with garlic powder and Saucy Susan, a very sweet and piquant bottled peach-apricot sauce similar to the duck sauce from Chinese take-out restaurants. These ribs are his adult take on that dish. He starts by tossing the ribs with a spice blend that gives the meat nuanced depth of flavor beneath the sweet and sour glaze.

We use a couple of neat tricks to ensure the potatoes don't end up tasting like the ribs. It is important to line the pan with foil. Place the potatoes directly on the foil and the ribs on a wire rack that rests on top of the sheet pan. They roast together for an hour, at which point the potatoes are tender. You take them out of the oven and smash them (actually, you press them down with a spatula, but "smash" sounds more fun) while the ribs get glazed and finish cooking. (That takes about another 30 minutes.) When the ribs are ready, take the foil out of the pan, place the smashed potatoes back on it, and stick them under the broiler just long enough to get crunchy bits along the edges and heat through.

As with all ribs, they take a while to cook in order to get tender. So while the meal is super easy and uses only one pan, bear in mind that you'll need about 2 hours of cooking time.

Serve the ribs and potatoes with a crisp green salad dressed with Parsley Vinaigrette (recipe follows).

MAKES 4 SERVINGS

1. Preheat the oven to 350°F. Line a sheet pan with foil and coat the foil with cooking spray.
2. Combine the brown sugar, garlic powder, smoked paprika, chili powder, ginger, and ¾ teaspoon of the salt in a large bowl. Add the ribs and toss to coat thoroughly.
3. Combine the potatoes and oil in a separate bowl. Toss with the remaining ½ teaspoon salt and the pepper. Arrange the potatoes, cut

side down, on the foil. Set a wire rack slightly larger than the sheet pan over the potatoes and place the ribs on the rack and roast 1 hour.

4.  Meanwhile, combine the preserves, honey, and vinegar in a bowl; mix well.

5.  Remove the pan from the oven and carefully remove the wire rack with the ribs. Transfer the potatoes to a cutting board and place the rack back on the sheet pan. Roast for 15 minutes, brush the ribs with half of the apricot glaze, and roast 15 minutes more. Brush the ribs with the remaining glaze and roast until the ribs are shiny and tender, 15 to 20 minutes more. Remove the pan from the oven and transfer the ribs to a serving platter; loosely tent with foil.

6.  While the ribs cook with the glaze, "smash" the potatoes. Working with one potato at a time, place it cut side down on the counter. Lay a spatula flat on top of the potato (parallel to the counter) and press down. The edges will splay out but the potato will hold together. (If you press too hard, the potato won't hold together. It should look like a messy flower when you're done.)

7.  Position an oven rack 4 to 5 inches below the heat source and preheat the broiler.

8.  Pour off any liquid from the pan and discard the foil. Place the potatoes, cut side up, on the sheet pan; broil until they are browned along the edges and heated through, 2 to 3 minutes.

## PARSLEY VINAIGRETTE

1 tablespoon white wine vinegar

1 tablespoon chopped fresh parsley

1 teaspoon Dijon mustard

¼ teaspoon salt

¼ teaspoon ground black pepper

3 tablespoons olive oil

Combine the vinegar, parsley, mustard, salt, and pepper in a small bowl. Whisk in the oil until combined.

# MINTED LAMB BURGERS

TZATZIKI + PAN-SEARED ARTICHOKES

## TZATZIKI

1 medium English cucumber, peeled, shredded, and squeezed dry

1 garlic clove, very finely minced

1 cup 2% plain Greek yogurt

1 tablespoon extra virgin olive oil

⅛ teaspoon salt

---

1½ pounds lean ground lamb

¼ cup finely chopped onion

½ cup fresh mint leaves, chopped

1 tablespoon tomato paste

¾ teaspoon salt, divided

¼ teaspoon ground black pepper, divided

3 garlic cloves

2 tablespoons extra virgin olive oil

2 (9-ounce) packages frozen artichoke hearts, thawed

1 teaspoon grated lemon zest

4 pita breads, top third trimmed off

4 lettuce leaves (Boston, romaine)

4 beefsteak tomato slices

SKILLET
GROUND LAMB

These deeply savory burgers are a welcome alternative to the usual beef burger. The tomato paste mixed in with the lamb does not impart a tomato flavor so much as a little acidity for balance, while the mint gives the burgers a bright note.

What better to go with a Greek-inspired burger than a little creamy tzatziki and pan-seared artichokes? You can serve the burgers sandwiched in the pita with lettuce, tomato, and tzatziki or serve everything on the plate and let everyone build their own sandwich—or eat the elements separately. (I like to dress the lettuce and tomatoes with tzatziki and eat my burgers with a fork; David thinks eating this any way other than in the pita is a sacrilege.)

**MAKES 4 SERVINGS**

1. Make the tzatziki: Combine the cucumber, garlic, yogurt, oil, and salt in a bowl.

2. Mix the lamb, onion, mint, tomato paste, ½ teaspoon of the salt, and ⅛ teaspoon of the pepper in a bowl; form the mixture into 4 patties, each about ¾ inch thick. Use the back of a spoon or your thumb to form a ¼-inch-deep indentation in the top of each patty.

3. Press the garlic cloves with the side of a knife blade to crack. Heat the oil in a large skillet over medium-high heat. Add the garlic and cook, stirring occasionally, until lightly browned, about 1½ minutes; remove the garlic and discard. Add the artichokes to the skillet and cook until lightly browned, 5 to 6 minutes. Stir in the lemon zest and the remaining ¼ teaspoon salt and ⅛ teaspoon pepper; transfer to a bowl.

4. Reduce the heat under the skillet to medium and add the lamb patties. Cook, turning once, until the burgers are browned and barely pink in the center and an instant-read thermometer inserted horizontally into the center of a patty registers 165°F, 12 to 14 minutes.

5. Serve the lamb burgers with the pita, lettuce, and tomato slices.

**WHY WE STICK OUR THUMBS IN OUR BURGERS**

*When burgers cook, they puff up in the center, which causes them to cook unevenly—and also to not fit well into buns or bread. Pressing an indentation into the center with your thumb (or the back of a spoon) ensures that as the center puffs, it doesn't dome higher than the rest of the burger.*

# LAMB CHOPS WITH ZA'ATAR

BULGUR WITH CRISPY KALE + BAKED TOMATOES WITH FETA

1 cup fine bulgur wheat

8 ounces kale, stems and thick center ribs removed, leaves cut into 1½-inch pieces

4 tablespoons extra virgin olive oil, divided

1¼ teaspoons salt, divided

4 plum tomatoes (about 1 pound), halved lengthwise

3 tablespoons crumbled feta cheese

2 mini (Persian) cucumbers, cut into ¼-inch dice (about 1 cup)

2 scallions, chopped (about ½ cup)

2 tablespoons fresh lemon juice

12 bone-in loin lamb chops, 1 inch thick (about 2 pounds)

1 tablespoon za'atar seasoning

SHEET PAN
LAMB CHOPS

Za'atar is an aromatic Middle Eastern spice blend with citrusy, earthy flavor. In the past few years, it has become more widely available in grocery and specialty stores (like Whole Foods). We sprinkle it over grilled vegetables and baked squash, and on all kinds of protein. It transforms these lamb chops into meaty hunks of concentrated flavor with almost no work.

Bulgur, which has a nutty flavor, is simply soaked in hot liquid and combined with crispy kale "chips," lemon juice, olive oil, and cucumber to make a refreshing and healthful salad. Baked tomatoes sprinkled with feta round out the meal.

**MAKES 4 SERVINGS**

1. Preheat the oven to 350°F. Coat a sheet pan with cooking spray.
2. Microwave 1¾ cups water until it comes to a boil. Place the bulgur in a bowl and pour the water over; let it stand until the liquid is absorbed, about 20 minutes.
3. Toss the kale in a bowl with 2 teaspoons of the oil and ⅛ teaspoon of the salt. Arrange the kale over two-thirds of the sheet pan. Toss the tomato halves with 1 teaspoon of the oil and ⅛ teaspoon of the salt. Place, cut side up, on the sheet pan. Roast for 15 minutes; toss the kale and top the tomatoes with the feta. Roast until the kale is crisp and the tomatoes are softened but hold their shape, about 10 minutes more.
4. Move the oven rack to 4 to 5 inches from the heat source and preheat the broiler.
5. Stir the bulgur and add 2 tablespoons of the oil, the cucumbers, scallions, lemon juice, and ½ teaspoon of the salt. Fold in three-quarters of the crispy kale. Just before serving, top the bulgur with the remaining kale.
6. Rub the lamb chops with the remaining 1 tablespoon oil and season with the za'atar and remaining ½ teaspoon salt. Arrange in a single layer on the baking sheet and broil, turning once, 7 to 8 minutes (for medium-rare).

# RED WINE-BRAISED LAMB SHANKS

WHOLE WHEAT COUSCOUS

4 (1- to 1¼-pound) lamb shanks

¾ teaspoon salt, divided

¼ teaspoon ground black pepper

1 tablespoon olive oil

1 medium onion, chopped (about 1 cup)

2 garlic cloves, minced

2 celery stalks, cut into ½-inch dice (about 1 cup)

2 medium carrots, peeled and cut into ½-inch dice (about 1 cup)

1 teaspoon fresh thyme

½ cup dry red wine, such as Pinot Noir

1 (14.5-ounce) can petite diced tomatoes

½ cup unsalted chicken broth

1 cup whole wheat couscous

SKILLET
LAMB

Lamb shanks (which have a Flintstone-esque look) are slowly simmered in red wine and tomatoes until the rich meat is falling-off-the-bone tender. As a bonus, while it cooks, the lamb perfumes your home with a lusciously alluring aroma.

Making this meal takes very little active time, but it cooks for 2 hours—which makes it the perfect dish to prepare on a lazy, wintry Sunday afternoon.

The lamb is also ideally suited for entertaining because it is just as delicious when made ahead and reheated. The last step is to remove the succulent shanks and some of the rich broth from the skillet and stir in couscous to absorb the rest of the broth. That should be done just before serving.

**MAKES 4 SERVINGS**

1. Season the lamb shanks with ½ teaspoon of the salt and the pepper. Heat the oil in a large skillet over medium-high heat. Add the lamb and cook, turning occasionally, until the shanks are browned, 8 to 10 minutes. Transfer to a plate.

2. Reduce the heat to medium and add the onion, garlic, celery, carrots, and thyme; cook, stirring occasionally, until they are slightly softened, 3 to 4 minutes. Pour in the red wine, scraping up any browned bits from the bottom of the pan; bring it to a boil and let it reduce by about half, 2 to 3 minutes. Stir in the diced tomatoes, broth, and remaining ¼ teaspoon salt; bring to a boil and cook for 1 minute. Add the lamb shanks; cover, reduce the heat to medium-low, and simmer for 1 hour. Turn the shanks over, cover, and simmer until very tender, about 1 hour more.

3. Transfer the lamb shanks to a plate and cover with foil. Remove 1 cup of the sauce from the skillet and set aside. Stir the couscous into the skillet, cover, remove from the heat, and let it stand 5 minutes. Uncover the skillet and fluff the couscous with a fork.

4. Serve the lamb shanks on a bed of the couscous and spoon the reserved sauce over the lamb.

# 3

# FISH AND SHELLFISH

## FISH THERAPY

If you lack confidence or comfort when cooking fish and shellfish, you are not alone. When we teach fish classes to home cooks at the Institute of Culinary Education in New York City, it usually starts off like a therapy session. Our all-time favorite example of this was the sky-diving instructor who tremulously asked how he could be sure fish was cooked enough to be safe.

Here are the top concerns that arise over and over.

## HOW CAN I COOK FISH WITHOUT STINKING UP THE HOUSE?

First, please don't light a scented candle: that just covers up one scent with another, and you end up smelling both. Eww. Also, don't blame yourself or the fish. (We're back to the whole fish therapy thing, aren't we?) Sometimes, stink just happens. The technical (chemical) reason is boring, but suffice it to say it does not mean your fish is bad or too old or improperly cooked.

*Before* you start cooking—not once the fish is on the fire—turn on your vent and/or crack your windows. This helps prevent the odor from accumulating.

If you do end up with a smelly house, fill a small saucepan with an inch or two of white vinegar and bring it to a gentle simmer. Let it cook over low heat for about 1 hour—during which time you should see steam rising from the pan. (If you don't see steam, turn up the heat a little.) The vinegar clears out the scent of fish and leaves your house smelling a little like a salad. That, of course, is preferable to the smell of fish—and it lasts only a couple of hours. Fish aroma, on the other hand, can linger for 24 hours. Vinegar, by the way, also works to get rid of the smell of fresh paint. (Sadly, we have learned that it barely makes a dent in the smell of skunk.)

## HOW DO I KNOW IF MY FISH IS COOKED?

While there is an old rule that says you should cook it 10 minutes per inch of thickness, we think that's a little crazy: some fish is more dense than others, and different methods cook fish at different rates.

The best way to know fish is cooked enough but not too much is to take a peek inside. Use the tip of a knife to pry it apart at a seam between the flakes; you want it to look moist and, for most fish, barely translucent in the center. It will finish cooking by the time it gets to the table. (We cook cod and swordfish until they *just* lose translucency to ensure any parasites are destroyed.)

Also, most fish will easily flake when poked with a fork—but it will do that when it is overcooked, too. And since overcooked fish tends to be dry and flavorless, we prefer the peeking method.

## HOW DO I KNOW IF THE FISH I BUY IS GOOD?

When choosing fillets, look for taut, firm, smooth flesh. If the top of the fish has many small ridges, it is a sign the flesh is drying out (much like wrinkles on our faces as we age).

Smell the fish. While refrigeration and ice make odors harder to detect, if fish has an ammonia-like scent or reminds you of low tide, don't buy it.

Whole fish should have bright, not foggy, eyes.

If you are concerned about making sustainable choices, download the Seafood Watch app from the Monterey Bay Aquarium. When you are at the seafood counter, simply type the name of the fish into the app and it will let you know whether it is a good choice or one to avoid.

## WHAT SHOULD I DO WITH THE FISH WHEN I BRING IT HOME?

You can leave it in the paper wrapper for up to 1 day. Place it on a plate in the back of your refrigerator. (That's where the fridge is coldest.)

To keep it for up to 2 days, rewrap the fish in plastic wrap—and again, keep it in the back of your refrigerator.

If you are concerned about whether the fish is still good, smell it. If you detect a slight odor, rinse and pat it dry. If the odor is no longer there, it was on the wrapper. If it still smells off, toss it.

Despite what our mothers thought, fish freezes really well. Fatty fish like salmon is optimal for 2 to 3 months, while leaner fish can be frozen for up to 6 months. (After those times, the fish isn't "bad" and won't make you sick, but the texture and flavor won't be as good.) To freeze fillets, wrap each individual portion in a double layer of plastic wrap to ensure air can't get to it, then place the individual portions together in a freezer-worthy plastic bag. Don't forget to label the bag.

# SALMON BLTS

## LEMON-BASIL MAYO

⅓ cup canola mayonnaise

2 tablespoons chopped fresh basil

¾ teaspoon grated lemon zest

8 slices applewood-smoked bacon, cut in half

4 (½-inch-thick) slices beefsteak tomato

4 (6-ounce) skinless salmon fillets, about ¾ inch thick

¼ teaspoon salt

⅛ teaspoon ground black pepper

8 slices country-style sourdough bread

1 cup baby arugula

**SKILLET
SALMON**

The first really great salmon BLTs we ever had were at Lake Austin Spa outside of Austin, Texas. We go there once a year for our favorite "work" trip: David and I each give cooking demos on successive days and in return stay at the beautiful, tranquil spa for several days, eating wonderful healthful food, taking yoga classes, and kayaking on the scenic river. It's no wonder we associate this sandwich with feeling blissed out.

Then again, maybe it is the heady combination of rich salmon, meaty bacon, and creamy mayo that does it for us. Either way, it is a pleasure that something this easy to make is just this good.

Generally when we cook salmon, we want fillets from the center, where they are thicker and more evenly sized. But when making this sandwich, it is actually preferable to use thinner tail-end pieces, which more gracefully fit in a sandwich.

**MAKES 4 SERVINGS**

1.  Make the lemon-basil mayo: Combine the mayonnaise, basil, and lemon zest in a small bowl and set aside.
2.  Cook the bacon in a large skillet over medium heat until crisp, turning once, 6 to 7 minutes. Transfer to a plate lined with paper towels to drain.
3.  Pour off all but 2 teaspoons of fat from the skillet and return it to medium heat. Add the tomato slices and cook, turning once, until slightly softened, about 2 minutes. Transfer to a plate.
4.  Season the salmon with the salt and pepper and add the fillets to the skillet, skinned side up. Cook, turning once, until they are golden brown on both sides and barely translucent in the center, 8 to 10 minutes. Transfer to a plate.
5.  While the salmon cooks, toast the bread. Spread 4 toasted slices with the mayonnaise and top with the arugula, tomato, salmon, and bacon. Top with the remaining toast and serve.

# MAYONNAISE

Mayonnaise is a thing of beauty and pleasure, but that creamy lusciousness comes at a high price in calories and saturated fat.

We set up a blind taste testing for ourselves (yes, that is the sort of thing married food professionals think is fun) to choose—without bias—our favorite healthier mayonnaise. When it came to flavor and texture, Hellmann's* canola mayonnaise beat out the "light" and "low-fat" mayonnaises by leaps and bounds. It is not as low in calories as the others, but it has zero saturated fat and incomparable flavor.

## MAYONNAISE COMPARISON

Regular mayo: 90 calories and
   1.5 g saturated fat

Olive oil mayo: 60 calories and
   1 g saturated fat

Canola mayo: 40 calories and
   0 g saturated fat

Light mayo: 35 calories and
   0.5 g saturated fat

Light canola (Spectrum) mayo:
   35 calories and 0 g saturated fat

Low-fat mayo: 15 calories and
   0 g saturated fat

* We tried a number of brands and our top picks were Hellmann's and Whole Foods 365 brand, Unfortunately, the Whole Foods mayo had substantially more calories (110!) and saturated fat (1 g).

# SALMON ON TOMATO-JALAPEÑO JAM

**ZUCCHINI COUSCOUS**

3 tablespoons olive oil, divided

1 large zucchini (about 12 ounces), cut into ½-inch cubes (about 1¾ cups)

2 teaspoons grated lime zest

1 teaspoon salt, divided

1 cup couscous

4 (6-ounce) skin-on salmon fillets

⅛ teaspoon ground black pepper

1 medium onion, chopped (about 1 cup)

1 small jalapeño pepper, halved lengthwise, seeded, and thinly sliced across

1 tablespoon minced fresh ginger

1 (14.5-ounce) can crushed tomatoes

1 teaspoon honey

2 tablespoons coarsely chopped fresh cilantro

SKILLET
SALMON

Salmon is such a rich fish that it can stand up to the piquant bite of the ginger, sweet acidity of the tomato, and heat of the jalapeño in this sauce.

Jalapeños can be mild—or not! The only way to know is to take a tiny taste. Bear in mind that they lose a lot of their heat when cooked. This dish isn't meant to be spicy-hot; the heat just gives it a little background oomph.

We serve this jammy sauce under, not over, the salmon to ensure the skin stays crisp.

**MAKES 4 SERVINGS**

1. Heat 1 tablespoon of the oil in a large skillet over medium-high heat. Add the zucchini and cook, stirring occasionally, until lightly browned, 4 to 5 minutes. Transfer to a large bowl.

2. Add the lime zest, 1¼ cups water, and ¼ teaspoon of the salt to the skillet and bring to a boil over high heat. Stir in the couscous, cover, and remove from the heat; let stand 5 minutes. Fluff the grains with a fork and transfer to the bowl with the zucchini; stir in 1 tablespoon of the oil. Cover the bowl.

3. Season the salmon with ½ teaspoon of the salt and the pepper. Heat 1 teaspoon of the oil in the skillet over medium-high heat. Add the salmon, skin side down, and cook until the skin is golden and well crisped, about 5 minutes. (The fish will not be cooked through.) Transfer to a plate.

4. Pour off the salmon fat left in the pan. Heat the remaining 2 teaspoons oil over medium-high heat. Add the onion, jalapeño, and ginger and cook, stirring, until slightly softened, about 2 minutes. Stir in the tomatoes, honey, and remaining ¼ teaspoon salt and cook, stirring occasionally, until thickened, about 5 minutes. Reduce the heat to medium and place the salmon, skin side up, on top of the tomato mixture; gently simmer, uncovered, until the fish is barely translucent in the center, 5 to 7 minutes. Remove from the heat, sprinkle with the cilantro, and serve with the couscous.

**ISRAELI COUSCOUS, AKA PEARL COUSCOUS, AKA PTITIM**

*The story goes that in the 1950s, when rice was scarce in Israel, this product was invented as a replacement. It is made from hard wheat flour formed into balls and toasted. Toasting gives it a nutty flavor; the shape gives it a pleasant chewiness. It stands up well to baking and reheating.*

# GRAPEFRUIT AND PISTACHIO-CRUSTED SALMON

½ cup salted shelled pistachios, very finely chopped

3 tablespoons olive oil, divided

4 teaspoons honey

1 tablespoon grated grapefruit zest

1 teaspoon Dijon mustard

1 medium onion, chopped (about 1 cup)

1 cup Israeli (pearl) couscous

1½ cups unsalted chicken broth or water

1 teaspoon salt, divided

½ teaspoon ground black pepper, divided

4 garlic cloves, thinly sliced

1 pound spinach, thicker stems removed

4 (6-ounce) skin-on salmon fillets

SKILLET
SALMON

This unusual topping came out of some work we did for a client. David, who doesn't like grapefruit, was skeptical about the idea, but it turns out the combination of bitter grapefruit, sweet and nutty pistachios, and rich, fatty salmon is a knockout.

**MAKES 4 SERVINGS**

1. Preheat the oven to 350°F.
2. Combine the pistachios, 1 tablespoon of the oil, the honey, grapefruit zest, and mustard in a small bowl.
3. Heat 1 tablespoon of the oil in a large ovenproof skillet over medium-high heat. Add the onion and cook until slightly softened, 2 to 3 minutes. Add the couscous and cook, stirring often, until lightly toasted, about 2 minutes. Stir in the broth, ¼ teaspoon of the salt, and ⅛ teaspoon of the pepper; bring to a boil, reduce the heat to medium, cover, and simmer until the liquid has been absorbed, about 10 minutes. Transfer the couscous to a bowl.
4. Heat the remaining 1 tablespoon oil in the skillet over medium-high heat. Add the garlic and cook, stirring, until it starts to brown, about 1 minute. Stir in the spinach, ¼ teaspoon of the salt, and ⅛ teaspoon of the pepper and cook until it is just wilted. Transfer to a bowl.
5. Season the salmon with the remaining ½ teaspoon salt and ¼ teaspoon pepper. Heat the skillet over medium-high heat; add the salmon, skin side up, and cook until lightly browned, about 3 minutes.
6. Remove the salmon from the skillet and pour off any oil left in the pan; give it a quick wipe with a paper towel.
7. Return the salmon to the skillet, placing it to one side, skin side down. Spread the pistachio mixture evenly over the top of each fillet. Add the couscous and spinach to the skillet in two separate piles. Transfer to the oven and roast until the salmon is just translucent in the center, 8 to 10 minutes.

# SALMON WITH BOK CHOY AND RADISHES

RICE

2 (10-ounce) bags frozen brown (or white) rice

1 teaspoon olive oil

4 (6-ounce) skin-on salmon fillets

½ teaspoon salt

¼ teaspoon ground black pepper

¼ cup unsalted chicken broth

¼ cup dry white wine, such as Sauvignon Blanc

1 teaspoon Dijon mustard

4 baby bok choy (about 1 pound), halved lengthwise

8 radishes, quartered (about ⅔ cup)

2 garlic cloves, thinly sliced

SKILLET
SALMON

Cooking radishes mellows their spicy flavor—but thankfully doesn't completely eliminate it. The radishes are left with just enough sass to hold their own against rich, fatty salmon and mildly bitter bok choy. A simple pan sauce made with white wine, mustard, and broth ties the flavors all together.

We like to serve this with white or brown rice to make it a complete meal.

MAKES 4 SERVINGS

1. Microwave the rice according to package directions. Keep it warm in a covered bowl.

2. Heat the oil in a large skillet over medium heat. Season the salmon with the salt and pepper and add it to the skillet skin side up. Cook until it is lightly browned on the underside, about 3 minutes. Turn and cook until the skin is crisp but the fish is not yet fully cooked through, about 5 minutes more. Transfer to a plate.

3. Add the broth, wine, and mustard to the skillet; cook, stirring until the mustard dissolves, about 30 seconds. Add the bok choy, radishes, and garlic and cook until the bok choy is lightly browned on the underside, about 3 minutes. Turn the bok choy over and top with the salmon, skin side up; cover and continue cooking until the bok choy is crisp-tender at the base and the salmon is just translucent in the center, 2 to 3 minutes. Serve with the rice.

> ### WHAT'S THAT WHITE STUFF ON MY SALMON?
> *Anyone who has ever cooked salmon has experienced it: as the fish heats up, white globs start oozing out the sides. Most people assume it is fat . . . but it is not. In fact, the mild-tasting white stuff is a form of protein called albumin—related to but not the same as egg white—which is albumen with an E.*

# SWEET CHILI-GLAZED SALMON

SUGAR SNAPS + RICE

1 cup long-grain white rice

¾ teaspoon salt, divided

3 tablespoons sugar

1½ tablespoons fresh lime juice

1 tablespoon fish sauce

1½ teaspoons chili-garlic sauce

½ teaspoon cornstarch

12 ounces sugar snap peas

1 tablespoon olive oil

4 (6-ounce) skin-on salmon fillets

SHEET PAN
SALMON

Here it is: a recipe that requires absolutely no chopping and makes an entire, really tasty, well-balanced meal in just four incredibly quick steps. We're not overselling this, either. All you do is start the rice on the sheet pan, add the salmon brushed with a glaze you whisk together, and later add the sugar snaps.

MAKES 4 SERVINGS

1. Preheat the oven to 425°F. Coat a sheet pan with cooking spray.
2. Combine the rice, 2½ cups water, and ¼ teaspoon of the salt on the sheet pan. Bake for 20 minutes.
3. Meanwhile, whisk the sugar, lime juice, fish sauce, chili-garlic sauce, and cornstarch in a small bowl to make the glaze. Combine the sugar snaps with the oil and ¼ teaspoon of the salt in a separate bowl.
4. After the rice has cooked for 20 minutes, place the salmon, skin side down, on the sheet pan (directly on top of the rice). Season the fish with the remaining ¼ teaspoon salt and brush it with about one-third of the chili glaze. Roast for 5 minutes, again brush the salmon with about one-third of the glaze, and add the sugar snaps to the pan. Roast another 5 minutes and brush with the remaining glaze. Roast until the salmon is just translucent in the center and the sugar snaps are crisp-tender, about 5 minutes more.

# IS IT DONE?

We like to remove salmon from the heat—whether the oven or stove—when there is just a trace of translucency in the center. By the time it reaches the table, the translucency will be gone but the fish will be delectably moist and tender.

Here are three ways to judge the doneness of salmon:

- The outside color method: You don't want to cook the fish until the sides have turned completely white—you should see pink, but that pink will no longer look raw and translucent.

- The cheat method: To peek inside the fish, insert the tip of a sharp knife directly into the top of the fish along an existing line in the flesh. Go straight down so you don't tear the flesh. Pull it open slightly, take a quick look, and close it back with your fingers. As long as you are careful and do it along an existing seam, no one will ever know.

- The touch method (the method chefs use; it is the best method but takes practice): Press the top of the fish lightly with your index finger. If it yields easily, it is likely still rare. If it is very firm, chances are it is overcooked. If you are right in between the two, then like Goldilocks, you've gotten it just right!

SWEET CHILI-GLAZED SALMON  158

# TILAPIA IN CRAZY WATER

1 tablespoon olive oil

4 garlic cloves, thinly sliced

3 cups cherry tomatoes

½ cup dry white wine, such as Sauvignon Blanc

¼ teaspoon dried thyme

¼ teaspoon fennel seeds

1 teaspoon salt, divided

¾ cup orzo pasta

3 tablespoons unsalted butter

4 (6-ounce) tilapia fillets

12 ounces sugar snap peas

SKILLET
TILAPIA

Crazy water is a translation from the Italian name for this very flavorful broth that is based on water. (It's crazy that water can taste this good, and that such a tasty broth can be this easy!) Much of the crazy water in this dish is absorbed by the orzo—but the base is still brothy enough to warrant serving in a shallow bowl or deep plate.

MAKES 4 SERVINGS

1. Heat the oil in a large skillet over medium-high heat. Add the garlic and cook, stirring, for 30 seconds. Add the cherry tomatoes and cook, shaking the pan occasionally, until the tomatoes just begin to wilt, 2 to 3 minutes. Add 4 cups water, the wine, thyme, fennel seeds, and ½ teaspoon of the salt and bring to a boil. Boil for 10 minutes to thicken the liquid slightly. Add the orzo and cook for 5 minutes. Reduce the heat to medium and simmer; swirl in the butter until it is melted.

2. Season the tilapia with the remaining ½ teaspoon salt. Place the fish on top of the orzo and simmer, uncovered, until it is nearly cooked through, about 8 minutes (depending on the size of your fillets). Add the sugar snaps, cover, and cook until the tilapia is opaque in the center and the sugar snaps are bright green and crisp-tender, about 3 minutes more.

## THE MYTH ABOUT TILAPIA

Tilapia suffers from an undeserved bad reputation, thanks to a sensationalist headline that made the rounds a few years ago. (It read "How Tilapia Is a More Unhealthy Food Than Bacon.") The bad reporting was based on the idea that tilapia, a lean fish, is low in healthy omega-3 fatty acids, the fats that make salmon so good for you. But just because it doesn't have those great omega-3s doesn't make it bad for you.

Tilapia is a low-calorie, affordable source of protein. The inflammatory article also claimed tilapia is bad for the environment. When we want to know whether a fish is a good choice for both human and environmental health, we check Monterey Bay Aquarium's Seafood Watch program. (You can download their app on your phone and use it while you stand at the fish counter.) The science-based organization agrees: this mild, flaky fish gets a thumbs-up rating for sustainability.

# BROILED HADDOCK SANDWICH

COLESLAW

⅔ cup canola mayonnaise, divided

2 tablespoons sweet pickle relish

2 tablespoons cider vinegar

1 tablespoon sugar

¾ teaspoon salt, divided

1 (8-ounce) bag shredded red cabbage (about 4 cups)

2 cups shredded carrots

4 (6-ounce) haddock fillets

1 tablespoon olive oil

¼ teaspoon ground black pepper

4 brioche hamburger buns

4 lettuce leaves (Boston, romaine)

4 beefsteak tomato slices

SHEET PAN
HADDOCK

There is something wonderful about a really good fish sandwich . . . one you can sink your teeth into, on a soft bun, not fishy but with the taste of an ocean breeze—and dripping with tartar sauce (mayonnaise laced with sweet pickles).

Haddock is ideal for fish sandwiches. It is a lean, mild white fish, in many ways similar to cod but with a softer, more fragile texture and a little more flavor. (Cod and haddock are interchangeable in most recipes, including this one.)

This entire dinner will take you all of about 15 minutes to prepare—and it eats like a real treat.

MAKES 4 SERVINGS

1. Position an oven rack 4 to 5 inches below the heat source and preheat the broiler. Coat a sheet pan with cooking spray.
2. Make the tartar sauce: Combine ⅓ cup of the mayonnaise and the relish in a small bowl.
3. Make the coleslaw: Combine the remaining ⅓ cup mayonnaise, the vinegar, sugar, and ¼ teaspoon of the salt in a bowl. Add the cabbage and carrots and toss well.
4. Rub the haddock fillets with the oil and season with the remaining ½ teaspoon salt and the pepper. Transfer to the sheet pan.
5. Broil the haddock until the fish just flakes but is still moist, 7 to 8 minutes.
6. To serve, spread the cut sides of each bun with the tartar sauce. Place lettuce, tomato, and fish on each bun bottom, cover with the bun tops, and serve with the coleslaw.

# NEW ENGLAND FISH DINNER

1 pound Yukon Gold potatoes, cut into ¾-inch chunks

1 medium onion, chopped (about 1 cup)

2 tablespoons olive oil, divided

1 teaspoon fresh thyme

1 teaspoon salt, divided

½ teaspoon ground black pepper, divided

12 ounces green beans, trimmed

4 (6-ounce) cod fillets

¾ cup panko breadcrumbs

2 tablespoons unsalted butter, melted

2 tablespoons chopped fresh parsley

1 teaspoon grated lemon zest

**SHEET PAN**
**COD**

Cod was our go-to fish when I was a child growing up in New England. (David, a New Yorker, grew up eating mostly flounder.) Cod was plentiful, and its mild flavor made it easy for us kids to like. My mother used to crust it with cornmeal and stick it under the broiler.

This is our updated crunchy-crusted version, coated with buttery, lemony panko and roasted with creamy Yukon Gold potatoes and crisp green beans. Flounder, haddock, pollock, and halibut all make good stand-ins for cod.

**MAKES 4 SERVINGS**

1. Preheat the oven to 425°F. Coat a sheet pan with cooking spray.
2. Combine the potatoes and onion with 1 tablespoon of the oil in a bowl. Toss with the thyme, ¼ teaspoon of the salt, and ¼ teaspoon of the pepper. Arrange on the sheet pan in a single layer.
3. Combine the green beans and the remaining 1 tablespoon oil in the same bowl. Toss with ¼ teaspoon of the salt.
4. Roast the potatoes until they just start to soften, about 10 minutes. Slide the potatoes to one side and add the green beans to the pan. Roast for 5 minutes more.
5. Meanwhile, season the cod fillets with the remaining ½ teaspoon salt and ¼ teaspoon pepper. Combine the panko, melted butter, parsley, and lemon zest in a bowl. Firmly press the mixture evenly onto the top of each cod fillet.
6. Slide the green beans and potatoes over to make room for the cod; coat the exposed portion of the baking sheet with cooking spray. Add the cod and roast until the potatoes are browned and the fish just flakes but is still moist, 14 to 15 minutes.

# TUNA PUTTANESCA

1¾ cups ditalini pasta (about 8 ounces)

1 teaspoon salt, divided

6 cups bite-size broccoli florets (about 1¼ pounds)

4 (6-ounce) tuna steaks

¼ teaspoon ground black pepper

4 tablespoons olive oil, divided

1 medium onion, diced (about 1 cup)

2 garlic cloves, minced, plus 4 garlic cloves, thinly sliced

1 oil-packed anchovy fillet, drained and minced

1 (14.5-ounce) can diced tomatoes

¼ cup pitted Kalamata olives, coarsely chopped

1 tablespoon drained nonpareil capers

⅛ teaspoon crushed red pepper flakes (or to taste)

2 tablespoons chopped fresh parsley

SKILLET
TUNA

I've been making tuna puttanesca, both at home and in my classes at the Institute of Culinary Education, for more than a decade. David figured out how to make it into a complete meal—without fuss and bother. To be super efficient with your time, while the ditalini cooks, prepare (chop and measure) your ingredients for the topping. The whole meal will take you about a half hour.

One of the beauties of this meal is that the timing is all worked out for you. You'll sit down to a hot meal of perfectly cooked tuna topped with lusty puttanesca and accompanied by garlicky ditalini and broccoli.

**MAKES 4 SERVINGS**

1. Combine the pasta, ½ teaspoon of the salt, and 4 cups water in a large skillet over medium-high heat. Bring it to a boil and cook, stirring often, until the pasta is nearly cooked through, about 16 minutes. Add the broccoli florets and cook until they are bright green and the pasta is tender but not all the water has evaporated, 2 to 3 minutes more. Transfer to a bowl and wipe out the skillet.

2. Season the tuna with ¼ teaspoon of the salt and the pepper. Heat 1 tablespoon of the oil in the skillet over medium-high heat; add the tuna and cook, turning once, 6 to 8 minutes for medium-rare to medium or 4 to 5 minutes for rare to medium-rare. (The fish will continue cooking a little more as it sits.) Transfer to a serving platter and cover with foil to keep warm.

3. Return the skillet to the heat and stir in the onion, minced garlic, and anchovy; cook, stirring, until the onion begins to soften, 1 to 2 minutes. Add the tomatoes, olives, capers, remaining ¼ teaspoon salt, and red pepper flakes and cook, stirring occasionally, until the tomatoes begin to break down, about 2 minutes. Stir in the parsley, spoon the mixture over the tuna, and cover again with the foil.

4. Wipe out the skillet with a paper towel and heat the remaining 3 tablespoons oil over medium-high heat. Add the sliced garlic and cook, stirring, until it starts to brown, about 1 minute. Stir in the reserved ditalini and broccoli and cook, stirring often, until heated through, 1 to 2 minutes. Serve with the tuna.

## WHAT IS PUTTANESCA?

Puttanesca is traditionally a pasta sauce. The Italian word *puttanesca* translates as "whorish" or "of, pertaining to, or characteristic of a prostitute." The story goes that puttanesca sauce got its name because it could be made by hungry prostitutes quickly and easily between clients. Another version is that the garlicky sauce was aromatic enough to cover up other, less pleasant odors. Yet another explanation is that the smell of the sauce cooking enticed clients in from the street.

There are culinary historians who doubt all these stories and believe it was actually created in the 1950s by a restaurant owner. We think you should pick whichever story you like best and keep making this irresistibly piquant, invigorating sauce to serve with whatever you choose.

# STRIPED BASS WITH OLIVE-ARTICHOKE SALAD

ROASTED FINGERLINGS + BRUSSELS SPROUTS

## OLIVE-ARTICHOKE SALAD

**8 bottled marinated artichoke heart quarters, coarsely chopped**

**½ cup pitted Kalamata olives, halved**

**½ cup pimiento-stuffed green olives, halved**

**1 tablespoon extra virgin olive oil**

**1 pound fingerling potatoes, halved lengthwise**

**3 tablespoons extra virgin olive oil, divided**

**¾ teaspoon salt, divided**

**¼ teaspoon ground black pepper, divided**

**12 ounces Brussels sprouts, trimmed and halved lengthwise**

**4 (6-ounce) striped bass fillets**

## SHEET PAN STRIPED BASS

Mild, meaty farmed striped bass is raised sustainably and without exposure to contaminants, which makes it as good a choice for the earth's health as it is for human health. Its firm but flaky texture stands up well to high-temperature roasting, and the mild, almost creamy flavor makes a lovely counterpoint to the robust flavors of the olive and artichoke salad.

This entire meal—the fish and olive-artichoke topping, creamy roast fingerling potatoes, and crisp-tender Brussels sprouts—takes about 35 minutes to prepare.

**MAKES 4 SERVINGS**

1. Preheat the oven to 425°F. Coat a sheet pan with cooking spray.
2. Make the olive-artichoke salad: Combine the artichoke hearts, olives, and oil in a bowl.
3. Toss the potatoes in a bowl with 1 tablespoon of the oil; add ¼ teaspoon of the salt, and ⅛ teaspoon of the pepper and toss thoroughly. Place the potatoes, cut side down, on the pan and roast for 10 minutes.
4. Meanwhile, toss the Brussels sprouts with 1 tablespoon of the oil and ¼ teaspoon of the salt.
5. After the potatoes have roasted for 10 minutes, add the Brussels sprouts to the sheet pan and roast 5 minutes more.
6. While the vegetables roast, rub the fillets with the remaining 1 tablespoon oil and season with the remaining ¼ teaspoon salt and ⅛ teaspoon pepper. Slide the vegetables to one side of the pan and add the fillets. Roast until the fish just flakes but is still moist, and the vegetables are tender, 11 to 12 minutes.
7. Serve the fish topped with the olive-artichoke salad and accompanied by the potatoes and Brussels sprouts.

# VEGETABLE-STEAMED FLOUNDER WITH AJVAR

## AJVAR

1 medium eggplant (about 12 ounces), halved lengthwise

2 medium red bell peppers, tops cut off, seeded

1 garlic clove, peeled

2 tablespoons fresh lemon juice

1½ teaspoons sweet paprika

3 tablespoons olive oil

¼ teaspoon salt

1 tablespoon olive oil

1 medium red onion, chopped (about 1 cup)

1 cup quick-cooking barley

¾ teaspoon salt, divided

1 large yellow squash (about 12 ounces), trimmed, quartered lengthwise, and cut into ¾-inch chunks (about 2 cups)

1 large zucchini (about 12 ounces), trimmed, quartered lengthwise, and cut into ¾-inch chunks (about 2 cups)

¼ teaspoon ground black pepper, divided

4 (6-ounce) flounder fillets

2 tablespoons chopped parsley

SKILLET
FLOUNDER

Ajvar is a garlicky eggplant and red pepper sauce that hails from the Balkans. It is a lavish sunset-orange color and its flavor is piquant, tangy, and a little sweet. The eggplant and red pepper are roasted or (as we have done here) microwaved until they are very tender and the cooked vegetables are pureed with lemon and paprika. Here, the sauce turns simple flounder fillets into a flavorful adventure.

**MAKES 4 SERVINGS**

1. Make the ajvar: Pierce the eggplant skin in several places with a fork. Combine the eggplant and bell peppers on a microwave-safe plate. Microwave on high until the vegetables are very tender, 16 to 18 minutes. Let the vegetables stand until they are cool enough to handle, about 5 minutes.

2. Scoop the eggplant flesh out of the skin with a spoon and transfer it to a blender with the bell peppers, garlic, lemon juice, paprika, oil, and salt; puree until smooth.

3. Heat the oil in a large skillet over medium-high heat. Add the onion and cook until it begins to soften, 2 to 3 minutes. Stir in the barley and cook, stirring, until it is lightly toasted, about 1 minute. Add 2 cups water and ¼ teaspoon of the salt. Cover the skillet, reduce the heat to medium, and simmer for 8 minutes. (It will be only partially cooked at this point.)

4. Meanwhile, season the squash and zucchini with ¼ teaspoon of the salt and ⅛ teaspoon of the pepper.

5. Arrange the squash in an even layer over the barley. Season the flounder fillets with the remaining ¼ teaspoon salt and ⅛ teaspoon pepper and set the fish on top of the vegetables. Cover the skillet and cook until the barley is cooked through, the vegetables are tender, and the fish just flakes but is still moist, 10 to 11 minutes.

6. Serve the fish topped with the ajvar and accompanied by the barley and vegetables. Sprinkle with the parsley.

# FLOUNDER EN PAPILLOTE

ZUCCHINI + POLENTA

18 grape tomatoes, halved

20 pitted Kalamata olives, halved lengthwise

8 large pimiento-stuffed green olives, halved lengthwise

Scant ¼ cup fresh basil, thinly sliced

1 tablespoon drained nonpareil capers

2 teaspoons grated orange zest

3 tablespoons extra virgin olive oil, divided

1 large zucchini (about 12 ounces), halved lengthwise and cut across into ½-inch-thick slices (about 1¾ cups)

½ teaspoon salt, divided

¼ teaspoon ground black pepper, divided

4 (6-ounce) flounder fillets

1 (18-ounce) log precooked polenta, cut across into 12 slices

SHEET PAN
FLOUNDER

There are two really good reasons to cook fish in packets. The first is that your fish steams, so it stays moist and tender. The second is that there is *no* cleanup. None. The sheet pan on which you put the packets often doesn't even get dirty. How great is that?

You can't cook anything and everything in packets, but fish—especially mild white fish like flounder—is very well suited to it. As the flounder steams, it is infused with flavors from the other ingredients in the packet—in this case, olives, orange, capers, and tomatoes. The slices of polenta against which the fish is nestled also absorb other flavors in the packet, but without losing their own sweet nuttiness.

**MAKES 4 SERVINGS**

1. Preheat the oven to 450°F.
2. Combine the tomatoes, olives, basil, capers, orange zest, and 1 tablespoon of the oil in a bowl.
3. Combine the zucchini with 1 tablespoon of the oil in a bowl. Toss with ¼ teaspoon of the salt and ⅛ teaspoon of the pepper.
4. Rub the flounder fillets with the remaining 1 tablespoon oil and season with the remaining ¼ teaspoon salt and ⅛ teaspoon pepper.
5. Cut off 4 (18-inch) lengths of foil. Working with one sheet at a time, coat one side with cooking spray. Fold each in half (short end to short end) and unfold. All the food will go on one half of the foil. First, line 3 slices of polenta up in a row about 1 inch from the crease. Arrange the zucchini next to it and rest the fish over the polenta and zucchini. Top with the olive mixture. Fold the foil closed and crimp the edges all the way around to seal the packet. Repeat with the remaining foil and ingredients. Place the packets on a sheet pan.
6. Roast until the packets are puffed and the flounder is cooked through, 16 to 18 minutes.
7. Transfer each packet to a plate and carefully cut open the top to allow the steam to escape.

# ORANGE AND HERB-ROASTED BRANZINI

TOMATO, FENNEL, AND POTATO TIAN

2 russet potatoes (about 1 pound), scrubbed and cut across into ¼-inch-thick slices

4 tablespoons olive oil, divided

1 teaspoon salt, divided

½ teaspoon ground black pepper, divided

1 large fennel bulb (about 1 pound), trimmed, cut vertically into 12 (¼-inch-thick) wedges

2 beefsteak tomatoes (about 1 pound), cut into 6 slices each

2 (2-pound) whole branzini, cleaned, heads and tails removed

½ large navel orange, cut into 8 half-moon slices

6 fresh parsley sprigs

Lemon wedges, for serving (optional)

SHEET PAN
BRANZINO

Branzino, also known as Mediterranean sea bass or *loup de mer,* has firm, white flesh and a delicate flavor. It is responsibly farmed. Your fishmonger will weigh it before removing the head, guts, gills, fins, and scales; a 2-pound fish is the perfect size for two people.

We often roast the fish with the head and tail on, because we prefer the presentation, but it adds extra steps to the filleting, and many people are uncomfortable seeing the whole fish. The recipe—and the resulting sweet, mild flavor—is the same either way.

MAKES 4 SERVINGS

1. Preheat the oven to 500°F. Coat a sheet pan with cooking spray.
2. Combine the potato slices 1 tablespoon of the oil in a bowl. Toss with ¼ teaspoon of the salt and ⅛ teaspoon of the pepper. Arrange the slices on the sheet pan in a single layer. Roast the potatoes for 10 minutes.
3. Meanwhile, brush the fennel and tomato slices with 2 tablespoons of the oil and sprinkle with ¼ teaspoon of the salt and ⅛ teaspoon of the pepper.
4. Layer the potatoes, fennel, and tomatoes in two long rows along either side of the sheet pan. (Tongs or a spatula makes it easy to handle the hot potato slices.) Roast for 5 minutes.
5. Meanwhile, rub the branzini with the remaining 1 tablespoon oil and sprinkle with the remaining ½ teaspoon salt and ¼ teaspoon pepper. Fill each cavity with 4 orange slices and 3 parsley sprigs.
6. Place the branzini on the sheet pan and roast until the fish just flakes but is still moist, 18 to 20 minutes. Gently remove the fillets from the bones and serve with the layered vegetables and lemon wedges, if desired.

# HOW TO FILLET A FISH

1. Assuming you are starting with a fish that was roasted without the head or tail, place the fish on your board with the backbone facing you. Holding your knife parallel to the counter, slide the point in at the head end just above the backbone, about halfway between the top surface and the bottom so the bottom of the blade lies on the backbone.

2. Cut through the flesh, keeping your knife resting against the backbone. Use a spatula to lift the fillet off the fish and place it on a plate.

3. Now comes the rewarding part: Lift the skeleton up in the air and remove it all in one piece. But you're not finished yet.

4. The annoying little pin bones are still lurking along the outer edge of the fillets. (That is, the long edge opposite the backbone.) Use the blade of your knife to gently push the entire fatty/bony section away from the fillet. Use your fingertips (most efficient) or the back of a spoon (trickier, but better if guests are watching) to find any straggler pin bones and lift them away.

# SIMPLE ROAST SNAPPER

POTATOES + GRAPE TOMATOES

1 pound baby red potatoes, quartered

3 tablespoons olive oil, divided

1 teaspoon salt, divided

½ teaspoon ground black pepper, divided

1 pint red grape tomatoes

1 pint orange grape tomatoes

2 (12-ounce) skin-on red snapper fillets

1 tablespoon chopped fresh oregano

1 teaspoon grated lemon zest

SHEET PAN
RED SNAPPER

## GOOD TO KNOW

*To get a beautiful brown, crisp crust and creamy, soft interior, roast potatoes in an uncrowded single layer with a cut side down. (If you crowd them in the pan, they will steam and not get that gorgeous crust.)*

This dish is inspired by one of the best meals I've ever had. Years before I met David, when restaurant food was still mostly heavily sauced and garnished, I was on the coast of Portugal at a small restaurant overlooking the water. I ordered, and the gruff chef barked something to the waiter. The young boy ran across the street to the ocean, pulled in a net, deftly grabbed a live fish, and ran it back to the chef, who wordlessly filleted it and slapped it on his grill. I watched as he added a squeeze of lemon, a drizzle of olive oil, and a sprinkling of chopped fresh herbs. The tender fillet tasted of ocean air, its fresh, clean flavor highlighted by the simple seasoning. That meal taught me, in a deeply visceral way, the importance of respecting the inherent flavors of a good piece of fish.

We use this preparation with snapper, sea bass, and other mild white fish.

MAKES 4 SERVINGS

1. Preheat the oven to 425°F. Coat a sheet pan with cooking spray.

2. Toss the potatoes in a large bowl with 1 tablespoon of the oil; add ¼ teaspoon of the salt and ⅛ teaspoon of the pepper and toss thoroughly. Arrange them in a single layer on the sheet pan and roast for 5 minutes.

3. Meanwhile, combine the tomatoes and 1 tablespoon of the oil in the same bowl. Toss with ¼ teaspoon of the salt and ⅛ teaspoon of the pepper.

4. Add the tomatoes to the potatoes and roast for another 10 minutes.

5. While the vegetables cook, rub the snapper fillets with the remaining 1 tablespoon oil and season with the remaining ½ teaspoon salt and ¼ teaspoon pepper. Sprinkle the oregano and lemon zest over the fillets.

6. Push the potatoes and tomatoes to the sides of the pan and place the snapper in the center. Return to the oven and roast until the fish just flakes but is still moist and the potatoes are cooked through, 12 to 14 minutes more.

# HERB-MARINATED SHRIMP

1½ pounds peeled and deveined shrimp (16/20 per pound)

3 tablespoons olive oil, divided

½ cup packed fresh basil leaves, chopped

½ cup packed fresh parsley leaves, chopped

2 teaspoons grated lemon zest

6 slices bacon

5 garlic cloves, thinly sliced

1 (15-ounce) can cannellini beans, drained and rinsed

1 (5-ounce) package baby arugula (about 6 cups)

4 teaspoons fresh lemon juice

1 teaspoon Dijon mustard

½ teaspoon salt, divided

¼ teaspoon ground black pepper, divided

SKILLET
SHRIMP

Shrimp doesn't need much in order to be delicious. Here we play up its inherent briny-sweet flavor with a simple toss of basil, parsley, and lemon.

The real key to making great shrimp is in how long you cook it. Overcooked shrimp gets rubbery, and undercooked shrimp—well, that's just unhealthy and gross. When shrimp is cooked right, it doesn't curl up into a tiny little spiral (that's very overcooked), and it has what is called "snap." It's a lot like biting into a hot dog: you get that initial outer crunch of the skin before the piece snaps off. When shrimp this size are seared, all it takes is 1½ to 2 minutes per side to get snap perfection.

We've paired the shrimp with bacony, creamy white beans and the bite of wilted arugula and brought the whole dish together with a warm lemon-mustard vinaigrette—all in about 25 minutes.

**MAKES 4 SERVINGS**

1. Combine the shrimp, 1 tablespoon of the oil, the basil, parsley, and lemon zest in a bowl.

2. Cook the bacon in a large skillet over medium heat until crisp, 6 to 7 minutes. Transfer to a plate lined with paper towels to drain.

3. Pour off all but 1 tablespoon of the bacon fat from the skillet. Add 1 tablespoon of the oil and set over medium heat. Add the garlic and cook, stirring occasionally, until it starts to brown, 1 to 2 minutes. Stir in the beans and arugula and cook until the beans are hot and the arugula has wilted, about 2 minutes. Stir in the lemon juice, mustard, ¼ teaspoon of the salt, and ⅛ teaspoon of the pepper. Transfer to a bowl and crumble in the bacon.

4. Season the shrimp with the remaining ¼ teaspoon salt and ⅛ teaspoon pepper. Heat the remaining 1 tablespoon oil in the skillet over medium-high heat. Add half of the shrimp and cook until slightly browned and cooked through, 1½ to 2 minutes per side. Transfer the shrimp to a plate and repeat with the remaining shrimp.

## HOW TO BUY SHRIMP

One store may call those shrimp jumbo, another may label them large, and a third may deem them medium. It seems crazy that there is no uniformity in naming the size, but that's just the way it is. So what's a shopper to do?

It's actually very simple. All shrimp are also designated by two numbers, their "count." The count gives you the number of that size shrimp in 1 pound. So, for example, if shrimp is labeled 16/20, there are 16 to 20 of them per pound. The smaller the count, the larger and more expensive the shrimp. When we make shrimp as a main course for dinner, we typically buy 16/20s.

# SHRIMP WITH THAI COCONUT GREEN CURRY GLAZE

1 (12-ounce) russet potato, peeled and cut into ½-inch dice

8 ounces green beans, trimmed and halved

1½ pounds peeled and deveined shrimp (16/20 per pound)

¼ teaspoon salt

⅛ teaspoon ground black pepper

2 tablespoons canola oil, divided

1 medium onion, chopped (about 1 cup)

1 medium red bell pepper, cut into thin strips

2 garlic cloves, minced

1 tablespoon minced fresh ginger

¾ teaspoon jarred green curry paste

1 cup unsweetened coconut milk

1 tablespoon fish sauce

1 tablespoon light brown sugar

2 tablespoons chopped fresh cilantro

SKILLET
SHRIMP

While Indian curry relies on ground dried spices for its flavor, Thai curry is based on a paste made from spices and fresh herbs. Thai curry paste is sold in most grocery stores in small jars; it is often made with lemongrass and Thai ginger in addition to the usual herbs and spices.

For this dish, rather than drowning the shrimp and vegetables in a heavy coconut curry sauce, we created a glaze. It is a lighter, less cloying way of delivering the same zippy, pungent flavor.

**MAKES 4 SERVINGS**

1. Place the potato in a large skillet and fill with enough cold water to cover the dice by 1½ inches. Bring to a boil over medium-high heat and cook for 6 minutes, at which point the potatoes should be nearly done. Add the green beans and cook until they are crisp-tender and the potatoes are tender but still hold their shape, about 2 minutes more; drain.

2. Season the shrimp with the salt and pepper. Heat 1 tablespoon of the oil in the skillet over medium-high heat and add half the shrimp. Cook, turning once, until the shrimp are slightly browned and just cooked through, about 1½ minutes per side. Transfer them to a plate and repeat with the remaining shrimp.

3. Heat the remaining 1 tablespoon oil over medium-high heat. Add the onion, bell pepper, garlic, and ginger and cook until slightly softened, 2 to 3 minutes. Stir in the curry paste and cook, stirring, for 30 seconds.

4. Reduce the heat to medium and add the coconut milk, fish sauce, and brown sugar; bring to a simmer and cook, stirring occasionally, for 1 minute. Return the potatoes and green beans to the skillet and cook until heated through for 2 minutes. Add the shrimp and cook until heated through, 1 to 2 minutes. Remove the skillet from the heat and stir in the cilantro.

## SHRIMP IN THE PANTRY

We think of shrimp as a pantry item. We buy 2-pound zip-top bags of frozen shrimp when it is on sale and just pull out however much we need 20 minutes before we want to cook it. To thaw shrimp, place the frozen chunk of shrimp in a big bowl of very cold water. As it begins to thaw, pull the pieces apart, which helps it thaw more evenly and quickly. Within 20 minutes, the shrimp are thawed. Pat them dry and you're good to go.

We prefer to buy the shrimp already peeled, but if shell-on is a lot less expensive, our frugality wins out. Shell-on shrimp are often marked "EZ Peel," or the equivalent, which means the shell has been split, so that peeling them takes only minutes. (They come already deveined.)

# GREEK SHRIMP WITH FETA

POTATOES + ROASTED BROCCOLI

1 pound russet potatoes, peeled and cut into 1½-inch chunks

3 tablespoons extra virgin olive oil, divided

¾ teaspoon salt, divided

½ teaspoon ground black pepper, divided

5 cups broccoli florets (about 1 pound)

1½ pounds peeled and deveined shrimp (16/20 per pound)

1 garlic clove, grated on a Microplane

1 tablespoon fresh lemon juice

1 teaspoon dried oregano

¼ cup crumbled feta cheese

SHEET PAN
SHRIMP

It just doesn't get easier than this to get an entire meal on the table: you give the potatoes a head start on the sheet pan before adding the broccoli. You then toss the shrimp with fresh lemon juice and oregano, roast another few minutes, and sprinkle with feta cheese just before serving. Done—your tasty, healthful dinner is ready in less than 45 minutes!

**MAKES 4 SERVINGS**

1. Preheat the oven to 450°F. Coat a sheet pan with cooking spray.
2. Combine the potatoes with 1 tablespoon of the oil in a large bowl. Toss with ¼ teaspoon of the salt and ¼ teaspoon of the pepper. Spread the potatoes on the sheet pan in a single layer and roast for 15 minutes.
3. Meanwhile, combine the broccoli and 1 tablespoon of the oil in the same bowl. Toss with ¼ teaspoon of the salt and ⅛ teaspoon of the pepper.
4. Remove the sheet pan from the oven, turn the potatoes over, and slide them to one side of the pan. Add the broccoli and roast for 15 minutes.
5. While the vegetables cook, combine the shrimp, remaining 1 tablespoon oil, the garlic, lemon juice, oregano, and the remaining ¼ teaspoon salt and ⅛ teaspoon pepper in the bowl.
6. Slide the broccoli to the side of the sheet pan and add the shrimp. Roast until the shrimp are pink and cooked through, 5 to 7 minutes. Remove from the oven and sprinkle with the feta cheese.

# JAMBALAYA

2 tablespoons olive oil, divided

6 ounces fresh or frozen okra (1½ cups), cut across into ½-inch pieces

8 ounces andouille sausage, cut into ¼-inch-thick slices

1 medium onion, diced (about 1 cup)

4 garlic cloves, minced

1 medium green bell pepper, cut into ½-inch dice (about 1 cup)

2 celery stalks, diced (about 1 cup)

¾ teaspoon dried thyme

½ teaspoon dried oregano

⅛ teaspoon cayenne pepper

1 tablespoon tomato paste

1¾ cups unsalted chicken broth

1 (14.5-ounce) can petite diced tomatoes

1 tablespoon Louisiana-style hot sauce

½ teaspoon salt

1 cup long-grain white rice

1 pound peeled and deveined shrimp (16/20 per pound)

SKILLET
SHRIMP

Maybe it's that jambalaya is from the party-est place in the United States, but to us it's a dish that belongs at a lively, upbeat table. It's food for fun and sharing. We make it on weeknights (from start to finish, it takes about 45 minutes) and also when we have friends over. We make steps 1 and 2 in advance. When friends come over we pour the wine, put out some nibbles, and finish steps 3 and 4.

If your local grocery store has it, use andouille sausage, but kielbasa makes a very respectable—and tasty—stand-in.

**MAKES 4 SERVINGS**

1.  Heat 1 tablespoon of the oil in a large skillet over medium heat. Add the okra and cook, stirring occasionally, until the thin clear strings you see when you stir are no longer visible, 3 to 4 minutes. Transfer to a bowl and set aside.

2.  Heat the remaining 1 tablespoon oil in the skillet over medium heat. Add the sausage and cook until it is lightly browned, turning occasionally, about 4 minutes. Stir in the onion, garlic, bell pepper, celery, thyme, oregano, and cayenne and cook until the vegetables start to brown, 7 to 8 minutes.

3.  Add the tomato paste and cook, stirring, for 1 minute. Add the broth, diced tomatoes, hot sauce, reserved okra, and salt and bring to a boil. Stir in the rice, cover, reduce the heat to medium-low, and simmer until the liquid has been absorbed and the rice is tender, about 20 minutes.

4.  Stir in the shrimp, cover the pan, and cook until the shrimp are just cooked through, 4 to 5 minutes. (You'll know they're cooked through by color and touch: look for the inside curve to be opaque, not translucent, and the shrimp should be firm to the touch but not rubbery.) Remove the pan from the heat and allow it to stand, covered, for 10 minutes before serving.

# SHRIMP PANZANELLA

1 (12-ounce) loaf country sourdough bread (boule), cut into ¾-inch cubes (about 6 cups)

2 pints cherry tomatoes, assorted colors, halved

5 tablespoons extra virgin olive oil, divided

1 teaspoon salt, divided

½ teaspoon ground black pepper, divided

1½ pounds peeled and deveined shrimp (16/20 per pound)

1 English cucumber, peeled, halved lengthwise, and cut across into ½-inch-thick slices

1 small red onion, halved through the root end and thinly sliced (about ½ cup)

⅓ cup fresh basil leaves, thinly sliced

½ cup fresh parsley leaves, coarsely chopped

4 ounces fresh mozzarella, cut into ½-inch chunks

2 tablespoons red wine vinegar

SHEET PAN
SHRIMP

It seems that every cuisine that includes bread also has some kind of bread salad. These salads were no doubt created by frugal home cooks who needed to use up stale bread. In our household, stale bread simply doesn't exist—it gets eaten up too quickly. We "stale" it ourselves in this recipe by toasting it—but skip that step if you want or need to use up bread that is past its prime.

After you make the panzanella, if you have time to let it stand at room temperature for 15 minutes, the flavors will soak into (and soften) the bread, which makes this even more delicious. Serve panzanella at room temperature.

**MAKES 4 SERVINGS**

1. Preheat the oven to 425°F.
2. Arrange the bread cubes in a single layer on a sheet pan and bake until lightly browned and crisp, 9 to 10 minutes; transfer to a large bowl.
3. Combine the tomatoes, 1 tablespoon of the oil, ¼ teaspoon of the salt, and ⅛ teaspoon of the pepper in a large bowl. Coat the sheet pan with cooking spray and spread the tomatoes in an even layer. Roast until the tomatoes just start to wilt, 9 to 10 minutes. Transfer the tomatoes and any juices to the bowl with the bread.
4. Position an oven rack 4 to 5 inches from the heat source and preheat the broiler.
5. Combine the shrimp with 1 tablespoon of the oil in a bowl. Toss with ¼ teaspoon of the salt and ⅛ teaspoon of the pepper and arrange in a single layer on the sheet pan. Broil the shrimp for 2 minutes, turn, and broil until just cooked through, another 2 minutes.
6. Add the shrimp to the bread along with the cucumber, onion, basil, parsley, mozzarella, vinegar, and the remaining 3 tablespoons oil, ½ teaspoon salt, and ¼ teaspoon pepper. Toss well.

# PAELLA

12 ounces peeled and deveined shrimp (21/25 per pound)

¾ teaspoon salt, divided

¼ teaspoon ground black pepper, divided

3 tablespoons olive oil, divided

3 ounces cured chorizo sausage, thinly sliced

1 medium onion, chopped (about 1 cup)

6 garlic cloves, minced

2 plum tomatoes (about 8 ounces), seeded and diced (about ¾ cup)

1 teaspoon sweet paprika

¼ teaspoon saffron threads, lightly crushed

1 cup Arborio rice

¾ cup dry white wine, such as Sauvignon Blanc

3 cups unsalted chicken broth

½ cup frozen peas

24 mussels, scrubbed and debearded (see page 194)

⅔ cup fresh cilantro leaves, chopped (about ⅓ cup)

SKILLET
MUSSELS AND SHRIMP

Paella is, at its heart, a convivial way of eating. The custom is to set the paella pan in the middle of the table and let diners reach in and help themselves. To that end, we like to bring it to the table in the skillet in which it is cooked, with a cloth wrapped around the handle and a big spoon for dishing it out.

This version has the lush flavor elements of the traditional dish, but it is both simpler and faster to make. For a meatless version, omit the chorizo and use smoked paprika in place of the regular paprika.

**MAKES 4 SERVINGS**

1. Season the shrimp with ¼ teaspoon of the salt and ⅛ teaspoon of the pepper. Heat 2 tablespoons of the oil in a large skillet over medium-high heat. Add the shrimp to the skillet in a single layer and cook, turning once, until no longer translucent, about 2 minutes per side. Transfer to a plate.

2. Add the chorizo to the skillet and cook until it begins to brown, about 2 minutes; transfer to a plate.

3. Add the remaining 1 tablespoon oil to the skillet and stir in the onion and garlic; cook, stirring occasionally, for 1 minute. Add the tomatoes and cook until they begin to soften, about 1 minute. Add the paprika and saffron and cook, stirring, until it becomes fragrant, about 15 seconds. Add the rice and cook, stirring, for 30 seconds. Pour in the wine, bring to a boil, and cook, stirring, for 1 minute. Return the chorizo to the pan and add the broth and the remaining ½ teaspoon salt and ⅛ teaspoon pepper; reduce the heat to medium-low, cover, and simmer for 20 minutes.

4. Stir in the peas and nestle the mussels into the rice, hinge side down. Cover and simmer until the mussels open and the rice is tender, about 10 minutes. Remove the skillet from the heat; stir in the reserved shrimp and the cilantro, cover, and let stand 5 minutes.

# MUSSELS 101

Most mussels we buy are farmed, and there is nothing wrong with that. Mussels have been farmed successfully for centuries. Maybe that is because we humans have long been smart about them and known that they are highly nutritious. They are low in calories and saturated fat and high in iron and other nutrients.

## STORAGE

When you get mussels home, store them in the back of the refrigerator in a bowl and cover with a damp paper towel. (Do not store them in water!) They will keep well for a couple of days.

## BEARDS

These look like brown threads, or coarse hair, and are usually clumped together in one area on the side of the shell. If you can see a beard, pull it back and forth several times to pull it out. (Don't try to pull it straight out.) It's nothing gross; the beard is what the mussel uses to anchor itself (to, say, a rope if farmed).

## COOKING

**PREPARATION:** Before cooking, if any mussels are open, tap their shells lightly against the counter: they should close. That tells you they are alive—and they should be alive when you cook them. Think of it this way: They close up to protect against the horrific giant (you) knocking on their door. Rinse them briefly under cold water and pull out any visible beards.

**METHOD:** Be sure you steam, not boil, mussels. Steaming ensures they will be tender, plump, and tasty.

**TO SERVE:** Mussels will open up as they steam. Discard any that do not.

# SHEET PAN CLAMBAKE

12 ounces baby red potatoes

1 medium red onion, cut through the root end into 8 wedges

2 tablespoons olive oil, divided

1 teaspoon Old Bay seasoning, divided

1 pound shell-on shrimp (16/20 per pound)

3 ears of corn, husked, each cut into 4 pieces

1 large zucchini (about 12 ounces), cut into 1-inch chunks (about 2 cups)

¼ teaspoon salt

⅛ teaspoon ground black pepper

2 dozen littleneck clams, scrubbed

2 tablespoons unsalted butter, diced

SHEET PAN
CLAMS AND SHRIMP

As a second-generation New Englander, I think I know a thing or two about clambakes. And yes, I might be slightly biased about what they should look or feel like. So when David said he wanted to try—just try—making a sheet pan clambake, I was hesitant, to say the least.

I certainly didn't expect to fall madly, deeply in love with this far simpler, very healthful version of a clambake. One of my favorite things about it is that we can whip this meal together in no time, even on a weeknight and even in the dead of winter. And just like the clambakes of my childhood, this is fun to eat and share.

MAKES 4 SERVINGS

1.  Preheat the oven to 450°F. Coat a sheet pan with cooking spray.
2.  Combine the potatoes, onion, and 1 tablespoon of the oil in a large bowl. Toss with ½ teaspoon of the Old Bay seasoning. Transfer to the sheet pan and roast for 10 minutes.
3.  Meanwhile, toss the shrimp, corn, zucchini, and remaining 1 tablespoon oil in the same bowl. Stir in the remaining ½ teaspoon Old Bay seasoning, the salt, and pepper.
4.  Add the shrimp to the sheet pan along with the clams. Top with the diced butter. Roast until the vegetables are tender, the clams have opened, and the shrimp are cooked through, 17 to 18 minutes. Discard any clams that have not opened.

### WITH SILVER BELLS AND COCKLE SHELLS
*"Clam" refers to a large group of freshwater or saltwater bivalve mollusks, including razor clams, steamers, littlenecks, and cockles, to name just a few. Sweet, briny, and flavorful cockles are saltwater mollusks the size of a quarter, with symmetrical round shells that, enchantingly, look heart-shaped if viewed from the side. And thus the expression "You warm the cockles of my heart."*

# SKILLET LINGUINE WITH WHITE CLAM SAUCE

**SPINACH**

2 tablespoons extra virgin olive oil

8 garlic cloves, thinly sliced

2 shallots, chopped (about ½ cup)

½ teaspoon dried basil

⅛ teaspoon crushed red pepper flakes (or to taste)

1 cup dry white wine, such as Sauvignon Blanc

2 (10-ounce) cans whole baby clams, drained, liquid reserved

1 (8-ounce) bottle clam juice

12 ounces linguine

½ cup packed fresh parsley leaves, chopped

1 (6-ounce) bag baby spinach (about 8 cups)

2 tablespoons unsalted butter

SKILLET
CLAMS

It's easy to turn up one's nose at canned clams, but they can be like canned tomatoes—at times they add more to the dish than their fresh brethren. In fact, a lot of high-end restaurants use canned clams in their clam sauce and chowder, so we're in good company. The clams in the shell you see on top of the bowl of linguine are lovely, but they are a tasty garnish. The real flavor of the dish comes from clam broth. We discovered that by boiling the linguine directly in just the right proportion of bottled clam broth, wine, and water, we got even better clam flavor. Baby spinach adds a lovely grassy counterpoint and makes this 30-minute meal complete.

MAKES 4 SERVINGS

1. Heat the oil in a large skillet over medium heat. Add the garlic, shallots, basil, and red pepper flakes and cook, stirring occasionally, until the garlic and shallots are slightly softened, 3 to 4 minutes.

2. Increase the heat to medium-high and add the wine. Bring it to a boil and simmer for 1 minute. Add the reserved clam liquid, bottled clam juice, 2 cups water, and the linguine; bring to a boil and cook, stirring often, until the pasta is just cooked and most of the liquid has been absorbed, about 14 minutes. Stir in the clams and parsley and cook until heated through, about 1 minute. Add the spinach and butter, tossing until the spinach wilts and the butter has melted, 1 to 2 minutes.

## NO MORE GREENS GUILT

Do you buy triple-washed greens and then feel guilty if you don't give them a rinse at home? We, along with good science, hereby absolve you of all guilt. It turns out that washing those greens accomplishes nothing in terms of making them safer. They are washed under cleaner, more highly controlled conditions in the packaging plant than you could ever replicate at home. In fact, the minute you open the bag, they are more prone to cross-contamination than they were at the store. Please don't take this personally, but no matter how clean your house is, it is crawling with germs.

To help ensure the safety of greens:

- Before you buy, check the "sell by" date and take it seriously.

- Don't assume organic greens are safer. All the same precautions apply.

- If you notice any slimy leaves or liquid in the bag, toss the entire bag, even the leaves that look okay. That liquid is a breeding ground for bacteria, which can contaminate all the leaves.

But let's not end this little talk on such a downer note. The good news is that triple-washed greens really are clean!

# SEARED SCALLOPS WITH BACON-CHIVE VINAIGRETTE

RICE PILAF

5 slices bacon

1½ pounds dry sea scallops

¾ teaspoon salt, divided

¼ teaspoon ground black pepper, divided

3 tablespoons olive oil, divided

1 medium zucchini (about 8 ounces), halved lengthwise and cut across into ½-inch-thick slices

1 medium yellow squash (about 8 ounces), halved lengthwise and cut across into ½-inch-thick slices

1 medium red onion, chopped (about 1 cup)

1 cup long-grain white rice

BACON-CHIVE VINAIGRETTE

1 tablespoon white wine vinegar

1 tablespoon chopped fresh chives

2 teaspoons drained nonpareil capers, chopped

1 teaspoon Dijon mustard

¼ teaspoon salt

3 tablespoons reserved bacon fat

SKILLET
SCALLOPS

We love delicately sweet, tender scallops. Because they are so expensive, we make them only occasionally. When we do, we like to treat them with reverence—both in the cooking method we use and in the way we choose to dress them.

The method below combines the best of both worlds: Searing the scallops gives them a beautiful golden crust, and steaming them (to gently finish the cooking) keeps them tender and moist. Ideally, they should be removed from the heat when they still have a small line of translucency in the center.

Because we want their subtle flavor and lovely texture to be the star of the plate, we pair them with a light sauce. This mildly smoky bacon vinaigrette adds a little savory depth to the plate without taking center stage.

We serve this bacon vinaigrette on many other dishes: we drizzle it over sliced summer tomatoes, spoon it on grilled or roasted fish and more. Remember next time you cook bacon to save that tasty bacon fat! A little adds a lot of flavor, and it keeps well in the refrigerator for several weeks.

**MAKES 4 SERVINGS**

1. Cook the bacon in a large skillet over medium heat until crisp, turning occasionally, 6 to 7 minutes. Transfer to a plate lined with paper towels to drain; crumble when it is cool enough to handle. Pour 3 tablespoons of the fat into a microwave-safe bowl or measuring cup for the dressing and save the rest for future use (or discard it).

2. Season the scallops with ¼ teaspoon of the salt and ⅛ teaspoon of the pepper. Add 1 tablespoon of the oil to the skillet and heat over medium-high heat. Add half of the scallops to the skillet and cook without stirring until well browned on the underside but not cooked

*(recipe continues on page 203)*

through, about 2 minutes. Transfer to a plate. Heat 1 tablespoon of the oil in the skillet and add the remaining scallops, again cooking until they are well browned on the underside, about 2 minutes. Transfer them to the plate.

3. Heat the remaining 1 tablespoon oil in the skillet over medium-high heat. Add the zucchini, yellow squash, ¼ teaspoon of the salt, and the remaining ⅛ teaspoon of the pepper and cook until the vegetables are lightly browned, about 1 minute per side. Transfer to the plate with the scallops.

4. Reduce the heat to medium and add the onion; cook, stirring occasionally, until slightly softened, 2 to 3 minutes. Add the rice and cook, stirring, until lightly toasted, about 1 minute. Add 2¼ cups water and the remaining ¼ teaspoon of salt. Bring the water to a boil, cover, reduce the heat to medium-low, and simmer for 15 minutes. (The rice will be nearly but not fully cooked.) Top the rice with the vegetables and scallops, browned side up, cover, and cook until the water is absorbed and the scallops and vegetables are cooked through, about 5 minutes. Remove from the heat.

5. While the rice cooks, make the vinaigrette: Combine the vinegar, chives, capers, mustard, and salt in a bowl. Warm the reserved bacon fat (or bacon fat + olive oil to equal 3 tablespoons) in the microwave for 10 to 15 seconds and slowly whisk it into the vinegar mixture.

6. Spoon the vinaigrette over the scallops, sprinkle with the bacon, and serve with the rice and vegetables.

## DRY VERSUS WET SCALLOPS

Many scallops you buy are "wet," which is a nice way of saying they have been soaked in a sodium phosphate solution that both makes them look whiter and plumps them up. But as soon as those plumped scallops hit the hot pan, all the moisture they are retaining begins to leach out—which prevents them from searing.

It is crazy that when you buy wet scallops, which are sold by weight, you are paying for all that retained water. (It amazes us that the practice of plumping scallops is even legal, but it is.) Your fishmonger must disclose whether his scallops are wet or dry. Dry scallops are more expensive per pound, but you get what you pay for: sweet, fresh, and pure flavor, not scallops plus treated water.

# 4

# MEATLESS

## THE MAGIC OF UMAMI

For the sake of our health and the good of our planet, it is generally agreed that we should all be trying to eat more plant-based meals. To make meatless meals just as satisfying as those with animal proteins, we include foods with lots of *umami*, or savory goodness. The meaty flavor that makes steak, poultry, and other animal proteins so satisfying comes from a naturally occurring chemical called glutamate. Meatless foods high in glutamate/umami include:

- Soy foods like tofu and edamame
- Fermented and aged foods, including soy sauce, miso, and aged cheeses like Parmesan and Roquefort
- Certain vegetables, including mushrooms, seaweed, asparagus, tomatoes, peas, corn, and onions
- Slow-roasted and dried foods, such as sun-dried or roasted tomatoes and dried mushrooms

In addition, some foods, particularly spices, don't have umami but accentuate it, including smoked paprika, cumin, caraway seeds, and coriander.

# SHAKSHUKA

¼ cup extra virgin olive oil

1 large red bell pepper, cut into ½-inch pieces (about 1½ cups)

1 large green bell pepper, cut into ½-inch pieces (about 1½ cups)

1 medium onion, chopped (about 1 cup)

4 garlic cloves, minced

1 tablespoon paprika

1 teaspoon ground cumin

⅛ to ¼ teaspoon cayenne pepper (or to taste)

1 (28-ounce) can crushed tomatoes

¾ teaspoon salt, divided

1 (5-ounce) package baby spinach (about 6 cups)

1 cup crumbled feta cheese (about 4 ounces), divided

8 large eggs

SKILLET
EGGS

The first time I had shakshuka I was on a gastronomic tour of Israel, during which I stuffed myself silly on ethereal hummus, beautiful vegetable salads, and *sabich*, pita filled with eggplant, egg, and potato. Each night when I got back to the room, I called David to gush about the incredible food. But of all the dishes I had, shakshuka was my favorite. The juxtaposition of gently coddled soft-cooked eggs in a robust (and often fiery) sauce is part of its great appeal. The rich yolks temper the acidity of the tomato-based sauce and soothe the fire from the chile pepper.

In our version, spinach gives the dish textural and flavor variation (not to mention nutrients!), and crumbled feta adds a touch of appealing saltiness.

Serve shakshuka with a crusty baguette to sop up all the sauce—it's one of the best parts of the dish.

MAKES 4 SERVINGS

1. Preheat the oven to 375°F.

2. Heat the oil in a large ovenproof skillet over medium heat. Add the bell peppers, onion, and garlic and cook, stirring occasionally, until the vegetables are very soft, 14 to 15 minutes. Stir in the paprika, cumin, and cayenne and cook to combine for 1 minute.

3. Stir in the tomatoes and ½ teaspoon of the salt. Bring to a simmer, reduce the heat to medium-low, and cook, stirring occasionally, until the sauce has thickened, 14 to 15 minutes. Add the spinach and cook until it is wilted and bright green, about 2 minutes. Stir in ½ cup of the feta cheese.

4. With the back of a large spoon, and working one at a time, make 8 equally spaced indentations, or wells, in the top of the sauce. As soon as each indentation is made, crack an egg into it. When all 8 eggs are nestled in the sauce, sprinkle them with the remaining ¼ teaspoon salt.

5. Transfer the skillet to the oven and bake until the egg whites are just set and the yolks are still runny, 8 to 10 minutes.

6. Remove the skillet from the oven and sprinkle the top with the remaining ½ cup feta cheese.

## WHO INVENTED SHAKSHUKA?

Countries throughout the Middle East and North Africa claim shakshuka as their own. A Moroccan friend of ours swears it originated in his homeland, Tunisians are certain it is theirs, and Israelis point out that they are the ones who made this dish known throughout the world.

We understand; we'd like to lay claim to this skillet full of deliciousness, too. Instead, we'll just appreciate that it serves as a basis for many a fast and wonderful dinner—and often with variations. In this version we've added spinach and feta, but it can also be made with more diced vegetables in the tomato mixture, including zucchini and/or cauliflower. You can easily make wildly different–tasting versions by (for example) giving the tomato base Tex-Mex flair with jalapeño, lime, and cilantro; or Indian by starting with minced fresh ginger, cardamom, cumin, and coriander and swirling in chutney. You can also add leftover cooked grains to the base to make it heartier. The bottom line: Make this meal your own. Hey, you could even claim you invented it.

# ASPARAGUS, PEA, AND EGG PIZZA

1¼ cups whole-milk ricotta cheese

1 cup shredded extra-sharp provolone cheese

½ cup shredded whole-milk mozzarella cheese

½ cup loosely packed fresh basil leaves, thinly sliced

6 tablespoons grated Pecorino Romano cheese, divided

8 ounces asparagus, trimmed and cut into ¾-inch lengths

1 pint grape tomatoes, halved lengthwise

½ cup fresh or thawed frozen peas

1 tablespoon extra virgin olive oil

¼ teaspoon salt

⅛ teaspoon ground black pepper

1 pound pizza dough, homemade (page 121) or store-bought

4 large eggs

SHEET PAN
EGGS

Crunchy asparagus, the acidic burst of grape tomatoes, and runny egg yolks oozing over dough covered with a milky cheese spread is our idea of a perfect pizza. Our love for this dish is admittedly heightened by how incredibly easy it is to throw together.

You can make your own dough, which requires advance planning and a little more time and fuss, but who can argue against the pleasure of homemade crust? On the other hand, when life does not offer you an extra hour plus, there are several prepared doughs that make really good stand-ins. Your best option is to ask your local pizza joint to sell you 1 pound of their freshly made dough—we've never been turned down! Alternatively, look for a refrigerated yeast dough at your local market. (Whole Foods and Trader Joe's both sell good refrigerated pizza dough.)

**MAKES 4 SERVINGS**

1. Position a rack in the center of the oven and preheat the oven to 450°F. Coat a sheet pan with cooking spray.
2. Combine the ricotta, provolone, mozzarella, basil, and 4 tablespoons of the Romano in a bowl. Toss the asparagus, tomatoes, and peas with the oil, salt, and pepper in a separate bowl.
3. Place the dough on the sheet pan and stretch it to fit. (Work from the center outward so you don't get skinny, torn edges and a thick crust in the middle.) Spread the top of the dough with the ricotta mixture, leaving a ½-inch border around the edges. Top with the vegetable mixture and sprinkle with the remaining 2 tablespoons Romano. With the back of a spoon, make four 3-inch-wide indentations in the dough, one in each quadrant. (These are nests for the eggs.)
4. Bake the pizza for 10 minutes. The hollows you created will have puffed up a bit; press each one down with the back of the spoon again. Break an egg into each indentation. Return the pizza to the oven and bake it until the dough is cooked through and the eggs are set but the yolk is still somewhat runny, 7 to 8 minutes. Remove from the oven and let stand for 2 minutes before cutting.

# CHICKPEA-SWEET POTATO HASH AND EGGS

1 sweet potato (about 12 ounces), peeled and cut into ½-inch dice

2 tablespoons olive oil

1 (15-ounce) can low-sodium chickpeas, drained and rinsed

1 medium onion, chopped (about 1 cup)

1 medium red bell pepper, cut into ½-inch dice (about 1 cup)

1 medium green bell pepper, cut into ½-inch dice (about 1 cup)

½ teaspoon smoked paprika

½ teaspoon dried thyme

½ teaspoon salt

1 (5-ounce) package baby spinach (about 6 cups)

4 large eggs

SKILLET
CHICKPEAS AND EGGS

Is everything better with an egg on it? Certainly this hash would be delicious even without eggs, but the creamy, rich yolks spilling onto the crisp vegetables, mild and slightly minerally spinach, and tender sweet potatoes bring it to a whole new level. Smoked paprika adds a little savory depth; if you don't mind the dish no longer being strictly vegetarian, you can also get that umami hit with tiny bits of chorizo (don't overdo it, or the hash will be about the sausage instead of the vegetables) or a very finely minced anchovy.

MAKES 4 SERVINGS

1. Preheat the oven to 400°F.
2. Spread the sweet potato dice in a single layer on a plate, sprinkle with 1 tablespoon water, and microwave on high until fork-tender, about 3 minutes.
3. Heat the oil in a large ovenproof skillet over medium-high heat. Add the sweet potatoes in a single layer and cook, without moving, until they are browned on the underside, 3 to 4 minutes. Stir in the chickpeas, onion, bell peppers, paprika, thyme, and salt and cook, stirring occasionally, until the vegetables are slightly softened, 7 to 8 minutes. Add the spinach in batches and cook until it is wilted, about 2 minutes.
4. Make 4 shallow wells in the vegetable mixture with the back of a spoon and crack an egg in each. Place the skillet in the oven and bake until the egg whites are just set and the yolks are still runny, 5 to 7 minutes.

# SPINACH, EGG, AND FRUITED QUINOA BOWL

1 cup quinoa, rinsed under cold running water

½ cup orange juice

½ teaspoon salt

⅓ cup dried cranberries

⅓ cup golden raisins

4 large eggs

### SHERRY VINAIGRETTE

1 tablespoon sherry vinegar

1 teaspoon Dijon mustard

1 teaspoon honey

¼ teaspoon salt

¼ teaspoon ground black pepper

4 tablespoons extra virgin olive oil

1 (5-ounce) package baby spinach (about 6 cups)

1½ cups packaged shredded carrots or 3 medium carrots, peeled and shredded

1 medium English cucumber, peeled, halved lengthwise, and cut across into ¼-inch-thick slices (about 1½ cups)

¼ cup shelled unsalted raw pumpkin seeds (pepitas)

SHEET PAN
EGGS

While many "bowls" are fun to eat, they can be a slew of work, requiring that each ingredient be cooked separately (usually in several pans). When we set out to create a meatless dinner bowl from one pan, we discovered that quinoa cooks up to fluffy perfection in a sheet pan. We give it extra flavor by cooking it in a combination of water and orange juice with tart dried cranberries and sweet golden raisins. The eggs then cook in ramekins on the other side of the pan while we make a simple vinaigrette. All that's left is arranging it in bowls!

**MAKES 4 SERVINGS**

1. Preheat the oven to 425°F. Coat a large sheet pan with cooking spray.

2. Place the quinoa on the sheet pan. Combine 1¾ cups water, the orange juice, and salt and pour it over the quinoa. Sprinkle on the dried cranberries and raisins, spread the quinoa evenly across the pan, and cover it tightly with foil.

3. Bake until the quinoa has absorbed the liquid and is fluffy, about 30 minutes.

4. Meanwhile, coat 4 (6-ounce) ramekins or custard cups with cooking spray and crack an egg into each one.

5. Remove the foil, stir the quinoa, and push it to one side of the pan. Set the ramekins on the other side and place the foil back over the quinoa, leaving the eggs uncovered. Bake until the egg whites are set and the yolks are still creamy, 10 to 11 minutes.

6. Meanwhile, make the sherry vinaigrette: Combine the vinegar, mustard, honey, salt, and pepper in a bowl. Slowly whisk in the oil.

7. Toss the spinach with 1 tablespoon of the dressing. Divide the quinoa among four bowls and arrange an egg and some spinach, carrots, cucumber, and pumpkin seeds on top of each. Spoon the remaining dressing over each bowl.

# COCONUT MASALA VEGETABLE CURRY

1 tablespoon olive oil

1 medium onion, chopped (about 1 cup)

3 garlic cloves, minced

1 tablespoon minced fresh ginger

2 teaspoons curry powder

1 teaspoon garam masala

⅛ teaspoon cayenne pepper (or to taste)

3 plum tomatoes (about 12 ounces), seeded and chopped (about 1 cup)

1 medium red bell pepper, chopped (about 1 cup)

1 medium sweet potato (about 12 ounces), peeled and cut into ¾-inch chunks

2 (15-ounce) cans low-sodium chickpeas, drained and rinsed

1 (14-ounce) can unsweetened coconut milk

1 tablespoon sugar

1 (5-ounce) package baby spinach (about 6 cups)

1 tablespoon fresh lime juice

1 tablespoon chopped fresh mint

¾ teaspoon salt

SKILLET
CHICKPEAS

This heady stew is as flavorful as it is colorful, thanks to two spice blends: garam masala and curry powder. Garam masala, which is sold in the spice aisle of most grocery stores, is made with sweeter spices, such as cinnamon, nutmeg, and cardamom. Curry powder, which gets its signature golden color from turmeric, is generally made with more pungent and savory spices, including coriander, cumin, fenugreek, ginger, and mustard.

Don't be put off by the long ingredients list for this dish. It requires only about 10 minutes of preparation and another 10 for active cooking. The end result is an opulent dish that tastes like it simmered all day.

**MAKES 4 SERVINGS**

1. Heat the oil in a large skillet over medium heat. Add the onion, garlic, and ginger and cook, stirring occasionally, until slightly softened, 3 to 4 minutes. Add the curry powder, garam masala, and cayenne and cook, stirring, for 1 minute. Stir in the tomatoes and cook until they begin to soften, about 2 minutes; add the bell pepper and sweet potato and cook until they begin to soften, about 3 minutes.
2. Stir in the chickpeas, coconut milk, and sugar; bring to a simmer, cover, reduce the heat to medium-low, and cook, stirring occasionally, until the stew is thickened and the sweet potato is tender, 14 to 15 minutes.
3. Add the spinach and cook until it is just wilted and bright green, about 2 minutes. Remove the pan from the heat and stir in the lime juice, mint, and salt.

> **HOW TO SEED A PLUM TOMATO**
> *Cut the tomato in half lengthwise. Squeeze each half as you would a lemon and the seeds pop right out.*

# ROASTED RATATOUILLE OVER GARLIC TOAST

4 (¾-inch-thick) slices country-style sourdough bread

5 tablespoons olive oil, divided

3 garlic cloves, divided

1 large eggplant (about 1½ pounds), cut into ¾-inch chunks (about 6 cups)

1 large red onion, chopped (about 1½ cups)

¾ teaspoon salt, divided

¼ teaspoon ground black pepper, divided

1 large zucchini (about 12 ounces), cut into ¾-inch cubes (about 2 cups)

1 large yellow squash (about 12 ounces), cut into ¾-inch cubes (about 2 cups)

1 medium red bell pepper, cut into ¾-inch dice (about 1 cup)

1 (14.5-ounce) can crushed tomatoes

1 (15-ounce) can low-sodium chickpeas, drained and rinsed

⅓ cup fresh basil leaves, thinly sliced

SHEET PAN
CHICKPEAS

There's an unwritten rule in our house: anytime we cook ratatouille, we double it to feed the freezer and store it in heavy-duty zip-top plastic bags. That's because this rich vegetable ragout can also be a pasta sauce, a topping for fish, a filling for roasted squash, a side dish, a main course, or a quick microwavable lunch. . . . It can serve endless purposes in the kitchen and at the table.

We especially love it mounded over garlic toast; the bread becomes as much of a treat as the ratatouille when it absorbs all the luscious flavors.

MAKES 4 SERVINGS

1. Preheat the oven to 425°F. Coat a sheet pan with cooking spray.
2. Brush the top surface of the bread with 1 tablespoon of the oil and place the slices oiled side up on the sheet pan. Toast until the bread is lightly golden, 6 to 7 minutes. Transfer it to a platter and rub the oiled surface of each slice with 1 of the garlic cloves. Mince the remaining 2 garlic cloves and set aside.
3. Combine the eggplant, onion, and 2 tablespoons of the oil in a bowl. Toss with ¼ teaspoon of the salt and ⅛ teaspoon of the pepper. Transfer to the sheet pan, roast for 15 minutes, and stir. Roast until the vegetables are tender but hold their shape, about 10 minutes more. Transfer to a large bowl.
4. Combine the zucchini, yellow squash, bell pepper, minced garlic, and remaining 2 tablespoons oil in the bowl. Toss with ¼ teaspoon of the salt and the remaining ⅛ teaspoon pepper and spread the vegetables evenly on the sheet pan. Roast for 15 minutes, stir, and roast until they are tender but still hold their shape, about 5 minutes more. Transfer to the bowl with the eggplant and add the crushed tomatoes and remaining ¼ teaspoon salt.
5. Spoon the mixture onto the sheet pan and roast, stirring once, until slightly thickened, about 15 minutes. Stir in the chickpeas and roast until heated through, about 5 minutes more. Remove from the oven and stir in the basil.
6. Serve the ratatouille over the garlic toast.

### CANNED BEANS: THE GOOD, THE BAD, AND THE UGLY

*Ordinary canned beans are outrageously high in sodium. Not only is it unhealthy, it makes the beans mealy—and you end up tasting mostly salt and not much bean.*

*We use only Goya low-sodium or organic canned beans (which are also low in sodium). They taste better, they are not mushy, and they are healthier. And, of course, we drain and rinse them under cold water. (Rinsing canned beans, by the way, reduces the sodium content by about another 30 percent.)*

# CUBAN RICE AND BEANS

## GREEN SALAD WITH SHERRY VINAIGRETTE

2 bell peppers, assorted colors, cut into thin strips

1 large onion, halved through the root end and thinly sliced (about 1½ cups)

3 garlic cloves, thinly sliced

1 tablespoon olive oil

1 teaspoon salt, divided

1 cup long-grain white rice

2 (15-ounce) cans low-sodium black beans, drained and rinsed

1 teaspoon ground cumin

1 teaspoon dried oregano

½ teaspoon ground fennel

½ teaspoon ground coriander

SHEET PAN
BEANS

Our kids don't want to hear the story again about how when David was a poor struggling student, he made a big batch of Cuban rice and beans and lived off it the entire week because that was all he could afford. So, kids, we won't tell that tale here.

Instead, we'll tell everyone about how this dish is so tasty and satisfying that you'll be happy to eat it for days, and so healthful and nutritious that you *should* eat it for days. And how it is so inexpensive and good to the earth that eating it for days is downright virtuous. (He told you so.)

Serve the rice and beans with hot sauce on the side and a crisp green salad with Sherry Vinaigrette (page 212). To reheat leftovers, sprinkle them with a little water and reheat in the microwave.

MAKES 4 SERVINGS

1. Preheat the oven to 400°F. Coat a sheet pan with cooking spray.
2. Combine the bell peppers, onion, garlic, and oil in a medium bowl. Toss with ¼ teaspoon of the salt. Spread the vegetables on the sheet pan and roast until somewhat softened, about 15 minutes. Remove the pan from the oven and stir.
3. Combine the rice, beans, cumin, oregano, fennel, coriander, remaining ¾ teaspoon salt, and 2½ cups water in a bowl. Pour the mixture onto the sheet pan, stir well, and cover with foil.
4. Bake until the water has been absorbed and the vegetables are tender, 28 to 30 minutes. Remove the pan from the oven and let it stand for 5 minutes. Remove the foil and fluff with a fork before serving.

# BLACK BEAN, KABOCHA, AND KALE RAGOUT

SOURDOUGH BREAD

3 tablespoons olive oil

1 medium onion, chopped (about 1 cup)

4 garlic cloves, minced

2 teaspoons chopped fresh thyme or ½ teaspoon dried

1 teaspoon dried oregano

12 ounces kale, center ribs removed and leaves cut into bite-size pieces

1 (2-pound) kabocha squash, peeled and cut into ¾-inch cubes (about 3 cups)

2 cups unsalted vegetable broth

1 (14.5-ounce) can fire-roasted diced tomatoes

1 cup (about 4 ounces) small egg bow-tie pasta

2 (15-ounce) cans low-sodium black beans, drained and rinsed

¾ teaspoon salt

¼ teaspoon ground black pepper

SKILLET
BEANS

Kabocha squash, also sold as Japanese winter squash or Japanese pumpkin, has a unique flavor and texture among winter squash. It gets creamy when cooked, and its flavor combines the natural sweetness of a sweet potato with the heartiness and depth of pumpkin. Having said that, if you can't find kabocha, you can certainly substitute butternut or even acorn squash.

We have found that at times we'll get a very creamy kabocha that nearly turns to puree as it cooks, and other times it holds its shape really well. We love this hearty dish either way and serve it with crusty sourdough bread.

**MAKES 4 TO 6 SERVINGS**

1. Heat the oil in a large skillet over medium-high heat. Add the onion, garlic, thyme, and oregano and cook, stirring occasionally, until the onion starts to soften, 2 to 3 minutes. Stir in the kale and cook, tossing, until it is wilted, 2 to 3 minutes. Add the squash and cook for 1 minute.

2. Stir in the broth, tomatoes, pasta, and 1½ cups water and bring to a boil. Reduce the heat to medium-low, cover, and simmer until the squash has started to soften but is not cooked through, about 10 minutes. Uncover the skillet, increase the heat to medium, and simmer, stirring often, until the squash is tender and the pasta is cooked through, 5 to 6 minutes. Stir in the beans, salt, and pepper and cook until it is heated through, 2 to 3 minutes more.

## ROCK IT, BABY
*To cut open a kabocha (or most round winter squash), place it flat on your work surface. Use your knife to score a shallow cut across the top. Rest your knife in the groove and gently rock it up and down to make the groove deeper and deeper. You can work in small sections at a time, and it will go fairly quickly (especially after you cut through to the seed pocket from the first area). It doesn't take brute strength, just a little pressure and patience.*

# OOEY GOOEY MAC AND CHEESE

4 tablespoons olive oil, divided

2 cups 1-inch cauliflower florets

2 cups 1-inch broccoli florets

¼ teaspoon salt

8 ounces elbow macaroni

2½ cups milk

¼ cup all-purpose flour

4 cups coarsely shredded Dubliner or other Cheddar cheese (about 8 ounces)

1½ cups panko breadcrumbs

¾ cup grated Parmesan cheese

SKILLET
PASTA

In the South, mac and cheese is a vegetable; in the Northeast, a starch. In our house, we call it dinner—as long as it has "stir-ins" to make it a balanced meal.

Use this basic version as a vehicle for all kinds of variations. Stir in leftover chicken, chunks of lobster, ham, or just vegetables, as we have done here. Or get adventurous and use more than one kind of cheese in the sauce. (Gruyère is one of our favorites.) Whatever you do, don't skip the panko topping—the buttery crunch on top of all that creaminess takes this mac and cheese to a whole new level.

For a quick, healthier weeknight version, we use Kerrygold reduced-fat Dubliner cheese. It has a nutty, slightly sharp, Cheddar-like flavor and melts beautifully into a smooth, creamy sauce. It is made with milk from grass-fed cows and, unlike many reduced-fat products, contains no weird gums or stabilizers.

**MAKES 4 SERVINGS**

1. Preheat the oven to 400°F.
2. Heat 1 tablespoon of the oil in a large ovenproof skillet over medium-high heat. Add the cauliflower, broccoli, salt, and ¼ cup water and cook, stirring often, until the water evaporates and the vegetables are crisp-tender, 4 to 5 minutes. Transfer to a bowl and set aside.
3. Combine 3 cups water and the macaroni in the skillet and bring to a boil over medium-high heat. Cook, stirring often, until the water is absorbed and the macaroni is just cooked through, 8 to 9 minutes.
4. Whisk ½ cup of the milk with the flour in a bowl until smooth; stir in the remaining milk. Pour the mixture into the skillet with the macaroni and cook, stirring, over medium heat until the sauce is the consistency of heavy cream, about 4 minutes. Remove the pan from the heat and stir in the Dubliner until the sauce is completely smooth. Return the vegetables to the pan and stir until well distributed.
5. Combine the panko, Parmesan, and remaining 3 tablespoons oil in a bowl, tossing until the panko is evenly coated. Sprinkle the mixture over the macaroni and bake until golden, 12 to 15 minutes. Serve hot.

# ORZO WITH PAN-ROASTED CHERRY TOMATOES, OLIVES, AND FETA

3 tablespoons extra virgin olive oil

2 pints cherry tomatoes, assorted colors

1 medium onion, chopped (about 1 cup)

5 garlic cloves, minced

1 tablespoon chopped fresh oregano or 1 teaspoon dried

1 teaspoon sugar

⅛ teaspoon crushed red pepper flakes (or to taste)

8 ounces orzo pasta (about 1¼ cups)

¾ teaspoon salt

4 cups baby spinach

¾ cup crumbled feta cheese

½ cup pitted Kalamata olives, halved

SKILLET
PASTA

From the time you walk in the kitchen to the moment you sit down with a big bowl of this easy-to-eat pasta dinner is about half an hour, including the (minimal) prep. It's the sort of dish you make when you've got something to do after dinner (soccer practice, anyone?) or when it's been the kind of day that deserves a nice, easy food hug.

MAKES 4 SERVINGS

1. Heat the oil in a large skillet over medium-high heat. Add the tomatoes and onion and cook, stirring occasionally, until the tomatoes begin to wilt, 3 to 4 minutes. Stir in the garlic, oregano, sugar, and red pepper flakes and cook until the tomatoes are fully softened, about 3 minutes.

2. Add the orzo, salt, and 5 cups water; bring to a boil and cook, stirring often, until the pasta is al dente and the liquid thickens, 14 to 15 minutes.

3. Stir in the spinach and cook until wilted, about 1 minute. Remove from the heat and stir in the feta cheese and olives.

### SUBSTITUTING DRIED HERBS FOR FRESH
While it doesn't *always* work, or work as well, to substitute dried for fresh herbs—and vice versa—you often can.
*For every 1 tablespoon of fresh herbs, use 1 teaspoon dried.*
That's a 3:1 ratio. Dried herbs tend to add more flavor to slow-simmered sauces and dishes that get cooked a little longer. The more robustly flavored fresh herbs (thyme, oregano, rosemary, and tarragon, to name a few) may be added early on in a long cooking process, while more delicate herbs (like parsley and cilantro) are generally cooked more briefly. These are not hard-and-fast rules (fresh basil, for one, is used both ways), but they tend to hold true.

# ROTINI WITH WHITE BEANS AND BROCCOLI RABE

3 tablespoons extra virgin olive oil

2 medium red onions, thinly sliced (about 2 cups)

6 garlic cloves, thinly sliced

¼ teaspoon crushed red pepper flakes (or to taste)

1 bunch broccoli rabe (about 1 pound), trimmed and chopped into 1½-inch pieces

8 ounces rotini pasta

¾ teaspoon salt

1 (15-ounce) can low-sodium cannellini beans, drained and rinsed

⅓ cup drained oil-packed sun-dried tomatoes, cut into scant ¼-inch-thick slices

⅓ cup grated Pecorino Romano cheese

2 tablespoons unsalted butter

SKILLET
BEANS

The only way in which broccoli rabe is related to broccoli is that they are both cruciferous vegetables. Beyond that, they look a little alike but taste remarkably different. Broccoli rabe is pungent (in the way that a turnip is) and often bitter; it assertively stakes its claim as the "alpha" in most pasta dishes.

Rather than fight it with other big flavors, we like to nestle it among creamy white beans, sweet caramelized onion, and demure pasta. Slivers of sun-dried tomatoes and a scattering of red pepper flakes give the dish dimension and interest.

You can also make a mellower and kid-friendly version of this dish by substituting 5 cups broccoli florets for the rabe. Either way, you'll end up with a wonderful dinner on the table in less than 30 minutes, and, of course, only one pan to clean.

**MAKES 4 SERVINGS**

1. Heat the oil in a large skillet over medium heat. Add the onions and cook, stirring occasionally, until they start to brown, 10 to 11 minutes. Stir in the garlic and red pepper flakes and cook for 2 minutes. Add the broccoli rabe and cook until it starts to wilt, about 3 minutes. Add the rotini, salt, and 4½ cups water; bring to a boil and cook, stirring often, until the rotini is al dente and the liquid thickens, 10 to 12 minutes.
2. Stir in the beans and sun-dried tomatoes and cook until heated through, about 2 minutes. Remove from the heat, add the Romano and butter, and stir until the butter melts.

## HOW TO THINLY SLICE AN ONION

Cut the top ¼ inch off the stem end, which gives you a flat, stable surface to keep the onion from rolling. Cut down through the center of the onion's root end, forming two halves with the root end still attached. Peel off the outer papery skin. Place both halves, flat side down, on your work surface.

Holding the root end of the onion and with the tip of your knife on the board on the far side of the onion, glide your knife forward and downward, cutting into and through the onion to form thin half-moon slices. (Keeping the tip of the knife on the board gives you stability and makes it easier to get nice, clean, thin slices.) Be as deliberate and slow as you need to be in order to have control. You will get sloppier if you try to rush, and faster with more practice.

# CACIO E PEPE WITH EDAMAME AND ASPARAGUS

12 ounces spaghetti

½ teaspoon salt

1 cup frozen shelled edamame

8 ounces asparagus, trimmed and cut into 1½-inch lengths

2 tablespoons extra virgin olive oil

2 tablespoons unsalted butter

⅔ cup grated Pecorino Romano cheese

1 teaspoon coarsely ground black pepper

SKILLET
EDAMAME

Cacio e pepe is the beloved Italian pasta dish enriched with just olive oil, a little butter, grated sharp cheese, and plenty of black pepper. In the classic version, you reserve some of the drained pasta cooking water to give body to the sauce. But in our one-pan dish, the cooking liquid is already in the skillet, and you simply swirl in the other ingredients.

We've added fresh green asparagus and earthy edamame to give the dish heft and make it a more balanced meal. Chickpeas make a great alternative to the edamame, if you prefer. Either way, this dinner you'll make over and over again is on the table in less than half an hour.

MAKES 4 SERVINGS

1. Combine the spaghetti, salt, and 6½ cups water in a large skillet; bring to a boil over medium-high heat. After the water has come to a boil, cook, stirring often, for 11 minutes. Stir in the edamame, return to a boil, and continue stirring for 3 minutes. Add the asparagus and cook until it is bright green and crisp-tender, the pasta is al dente, and there is just a little starchy liquid left in the pan, 2 to 3 minutes.
2. Remove the skillet from the heat and swirl in the oil and butter until it is melted. Add the Romano and pepper and mix until well distributed.

### GOOD TO KNOW
*Don't use regular finely ground pepper from a spice jar for this dish! One teaspoon of finely ground black pepper from the jar gives you far more peppery heat than 1 teaspoon chunkier freshly ground—and it would overwhelm all the other flavors. Freshly ground black pepper will have more robust flavor and a somewhat coarser, more uneven texture. You can also use store-bought pepper labeled "coarse ground."*

# SKILLET LASAGNA WITH CARAMELIZED ONIONS AND SPINACH

2 cups whole-milk or part-skim ricotta cheese

⅓ cup grated Pecorino Romano cheese

2 tablespoons olive oil

3 medium onions, chopped (about 3 cups)

4 garlic cloves, minced

1 teaspoon dried basil

1 teaspoon dried oregano

1 (10-ounce) package frozen chopped spinach, thawed and squeezed dry

1 (28-ounce) can crushed tomatoes

½ teaspoon salt

¼ teaspoon ground black pepper

8 ounces lasagna noodles, broken in half (across)

6 ounces whole-milk or part-skim mozzarella cheese, shredded

SKILLET
CHEESE

Classic lasagna is what we call "project" food. As much as we love it (like almost every other human we know), making lasagna is a time- and space-consuming project.

This skillet version tastes every bit as good—but is made so much more quickly, with absolutely none of the hassle. It doesn't cut into the same perfect squares as old-school lasagna, but we actually love the way the gooey cheese, spinach, and tomatoes ooze all over the plate.

This is the perfect dish when you're craving simple comfort food and don't have the bandwidth to fuss with the separate tasks of boiling the noodles, making the sauce, and layering and baking the casserole. I'm not sure we'll ever go back to making lasagna the old-school way again.

**MAKES 4 TO 6 SERVINGS**

1. Combine the ricotta and Romano cheeses in a bowl.
2. Heat the oil in a large skillet over medium heat. Add the onions and cook, stirring occasionally, until lightly golden, 11 to 12 minutes. Stir in the garlic, basil, and oregano and cook, stirring, for 1 minute. Add the spinach and cook for 1 minute more. Add the tomatoes, salt, pepper, and 3 cups water and bring to a simmer. Add the lasagna noodles and cook, stirring occasionally to submerge the noodles, until the sauce starts to thicken, about 10 minutes. Add 1 cup water, return to a simmer, and cook, stirring occasionally, until the noodles are al dente and the sauce thickens, 12 to 14 minutes. Remove from the heat.
3. Position an oven rack 4 to 5 inches below the heat source and preheat the broiler.
4. Let the lasagna cool for 3 minutes. Spoon the ricotta mixture evenly over the top and spread it in an even layer. Top with the mozzarella and broil until the mozzarella melts and starts to brown, 1 to 2 minutes. Let the lasagna stand for 10 minutes before serving.

# LINGUINE WITH PEPITA-SPINACH PESTO

**1 cup shelled raw pumpkin seeds (pepitas)**

**4 cups fresh spinach**

**1 cup fresh basil leaves**

**⅓ cup grated Pecorino Romano cheese**

**⅓ cup extra virgin olive oil**

**1 garlic clove, minced**

**½ teaspoon salt**

**1 tablespoon olive oil**

**1 medium onion, chopped (about 1 cup)**

**2 garlic cloves, minced**

**1 (15-ounce) can low-sodium chickpeas, drained and rinsed**

**2 plum tomatoes (about 8 ounces), seeded and chopped (about 1 cup)**

**8 ounces linguine pasta, broken in half**

**½ teaspoon salt**

**Grated Pecorino Romano cheese, for serving (optional)**

SKILLET
CHICKPEAS

We love that a quick sauce made in the blender can give a meal such an appealing and unique flavor. Make double the pesto to keep on hand; it keeps in the refrigerator for a couple of days, or in the freezer for a few months. We like to freeze it in ice cube trays and plop a cube of it in soup for an instant flavor bomb. The pesto, which can be made a day or two in advance, is also lovely when thinned with a little water and drizzled over halibut or cod.

**MAKES 4 SERVINGS**

1. Make the pesto: Heat a large skillet over medium heat. Add the pumpkin seeds and cook, shaking the pan often, until lightly toasted, about 5 minutes. Transfer to a bowl and cool for 5 minutes. Combine the pumpkin seeds, spinach, basil, Romano, olive oil, garlic, and salt in a blender or food processor and puree.

2. Heat the oil in the skillet over medium-high heat. Add the onion and cook until slightly softened, 3 to 4 minutes. Add the garlic and cook, stirring occasionally, for 1 minute. Stir in the chickpeas and tomatoes and cook until the tomatoes start to soften, about 2 minutes.

3. Add the linguine, salt, and 5 cups water and bring to a boil. Cook, stirring often, until the pasta is tender and very little liquid is left in the pan, 13 to 14 minutes. Remove from the heat and toss with the pesto. Top with Romano cheese, if desired.

# PEANUT-COCONUT NOODLES WITH TOFU

### PEANUT SAUCE

½ cup creamy *natural* peanut butter

½ cup unsweetened coconut milk

2 tablespoons lightly packed brown sugar

2 tablespoons fish sauce

2 teaspoons minced fresh ginger

---

1 tablespoon canola oil

1 pound extra-firm tofu, drained and cut into ½-inch cubes

8 ounces fettuccine pasta, broken in half

½ teaspoon salt

1 cup packaged shredded carrots or 2 medium carrots, peeled and shredded

6 ounces snow peas

2 scallions, cut into ¼-inch pieces

¼ cup salted peanuts, coarsely chopped

SKILLET
TOFU

Whether you're making dinner for finicky children (of any age), having a big party, or cooking on a busy weeknight, these rich and silky noodles fit the bill. We tossed them with cubes of lightly browned tofu, but you can make them your own with seared shrimp, leftover pork, or any other form of protein you like. Snow peas and preshredded carrots give the dish bright crunch and beautiful color with almost no work, and their shapes gracefully echo that of the noodles.

The peanut sauce has many other uses; it can be a dipping sauce for chicken or shrimp skewers, and a thinner version makes a great salad dressing.

**MAKES 4 SERVINGS**

1. Make the peanut sauce: Combine the peanut butter, coconut milk, brown sugar, fish sauce, and ginger in a blender; puree.
2. Heat the oil in a large skillet over medium-high heat. Add the tofu and cook, turning occasionally, until golden brown, about 8 minutes; transfer to a plate.
3. Add the fettuccine, salt, and 5 cups water to the skillet and bring to a boil. Cook, stirring often, until the pasta is nearly cooked through and very little liquid is left in the pan, 12 to 14 minutes. Stir in the carrots and snow peas and cook, stirring, until the snow peas are bright green, about 2 minutes. Add the peanut sauce and tofu and cook, tossing, until heated through, 1 to 2 minutes. Remove from the heat; stir in the scallions and sprinkle with the peanuts.

### A WORD ON "NATURAL" PEANUT BUTTER

*Natural probably does not mean what you think it does. Peanut butter can be labeled natural and contain sugar.*

*Here's why it matters: if you make this recipe with peanut butter labeled natural that contains sugar, it will be far too sweet. If you make it with peanut butter made only from peanuts and salt, it will be balanced and lovely.*

### READY-TO-EAT CHESTNUTS

*Skinned, cooked, and ready-to-eat chestnuts are widely available in grocery stores and online year-round. We prefer the ones sold in bags to those that are canned or bottled for their fresher taste, and choose only chestnuts packaged with no added ingredients. They are somewhat shelf stable, although once opened they should be refrigerated. When eaten right out of the bag, they have a crumbly, starchy texture that you either like or definitely do not. Depending on their size, ten small chestnuts (1¾ ounces) have from 90 to 100 calories, potassium, and a little vitamin C.*

# GOLDEN TOFU WITH CHESTNUTS

**BUTTERNUT SQUASH + BRUSSELS SPROUTS**

¼ cup pure maple syrup

2 tablespoons lower-sodium soy sauce

1 tablespoon balsamic vinegar

1 teaspoon ancho chile powder

Scant ⅛ teaspoon chipotle chile powder

3 tablespoons olive oil, divided

1 pound extra-firm tofu, drained and cut into 1-inch cubes

1 small butternut squash (1¼ pounds), peeled, seeded, and cut into 1-inch chunks (about 2 cups)

1 medium onion, chopped (about 1 cup)

12 ounces Brussels sprouts, trimmed and quartered

3 garlic cloves, minced

1 (3.5-ounce) package ready-to-eat chestnuts (½ cup)

2 tablespoons chopped fresh cilantro

SKILLET
TOFU

This is an intriguing and unexpected dish. The hushed and subtle interplay of crisp-skinned, pillowy tofu with the slightly bitter crunch of Brussels sprouts, creamy sweet potatoes, and nutty, starchy chestnuts is enhanced with a draping of maple syrup tinged with smoky heat.

**MAKES 4 SERVINGS**

1. Combine the maple syrup, soy sauce, vinegar, ancho powder, and chipotle powder in a small bowl.
2. Heat 1 tablespoon of the oil in a large skillet over medium-high heat. Add the tofu and cook, turning occasionally, until golden brown, about 8 minutes. Transfer to a large plate.
3. Heat 1 tablespoon of the oil in the skillet over medium-high heat and add the squash. Cook, stirring occasionally, until it starts to brown, about 4 minutes. Add ¾ cup water and cook until the water evaporates and the squash is tender, 5 to 6 minutes. Transfer to the plate with the tofu.
4. Heat the remaining 1 tablespoon oil in the skillet over medium-high heat. Add the onion and cook, stirring occasionally, until slightly softened, 2 to 3 minutes. Add the Brussels sprouts and garlic and cook until they start to brown, 2 to 3 minutes. Pour in ⅓ cup water and cook until evaporated, 1 to 2 minutes.
5. Stir in the tofu, squash, and chestnuts and cook until heated through, about 1 minute. Add the maple syrup mixture, bring to a boil, and cook, stirring, for 1 minute. Remove from the heat and stir in the cilantro.

# TOMATO, ZUCCHINI, AND PARMESAN FRISTRATA

1 tablespoon olive oil

12 large eggs

¾ cup milk

½ teaspoon salt

½ cup fresh basil leaves, chopped

4 plum tomatoes (about 1 pound), cut lengthwise into ¼-inch-thick slices

1 medium zucchini (about 10 ounces), cut into ½-inch dice (about 1½ cups)

10 (½-inch-thick) slices French baguette (5 to 6 ounces)

½ cup shredded Parmesan cheese

SKILLET
EGGS

Make this for dinner or make it for brunch. Make it as the main dish or make it as a side. But whatever you do, make it. Here's why: it is the love child of a frittata and a strata. We're talking about layers of bread soaked in a custardy egg-milk mixture and layered with sliced tomatoes and little nuggets of zucchini. Oh, yes, and let's top it with a heavy-handed sprinkling of grated Parmesan. Then we'll bake it until the edges get crispy and browned (try not to break them all off before you bring it to the table) and the cheese is all melty, and then we will sit down and try not to devour the entire thing ourselves.

**MAKES 6 SERVINGS**

1. Preheat the oven to 375°F. Oil the inside bottom and sides of a large skillet.

2. Whisk the eggs, milk, and salt in a bowl until fairly smooth. Stir in the basil.

3. Place half the tomato slices in the bottom of the skillet and top with the zucchini. Pour in the egg mixture. Place the bread in the skillet in a decorative pattern, turning it over once to completely coat it with the egg mixture. Arrange the remaining tomato slices on top and bake for 20 minutes. Remove from the oven, sprinkle with the Parmesan, and bake until the egg is set (a toothpick inserted into the center comes out clean) and the cheese is golden, about 20 minutes more.

4. Let the fristrata stand for 10 minutes before cutting it into wedges to serve.

# ROASTED VEGETABLE AND HUMMUS SANDWICHES

1 (1-pound) eggplant, cut across into 8 (½-inch-thick) slices

1 large zucchini (about 12 ounces), cut diagonally into 8 (½-inch-thick) slices

1 large red bell pepper, cut into 4 panels

3 tablespoons olive oil

½ teaspoon salt

¼ teaspoon ground black pepper

### HUMMUS

1 (15-ounce) can low-sodium chickpeas, drained and rinsed

¼ cup tahini paste

3 tablespoons fresh lemon juice

1 tablespoon olive oil

½ teaspoon salt

4 ciabatta rolls, split horizontally

### SHEET PAN
### CHICKPEAS

This is really three recipes in one. First there is a recipe for roasted vegetables (great for gatherings) that we also use to make a vegetable platter.

The second recipe is for our short-cut hummus. When we have a hummus emergency—and we all know those happen—this is how we whip up a quick batch. Depending on the brand and batch of your tahini (or how well you were able to mix the oils and solids before using it), you may have to tinker a bit with the consistency by adding a splash or two of water. The hummus should be the consistency of whipped cream cheese; it should spread easily but not be runny.

The third recipe is this seriously satisfying meatless meal. Experiment with your favorite vegetables: yellow squash, meaty beefsteak tomatoes, asparagus, and mushrooms are among the many others that work well.

**MAKES 4 SERVINGS**

1. Preheat the oven to 450°F. Coat a large sheet pan with cooking spray.

2. Arrange the eggplant, zucchini, and bell pepper in a single layer on the sheet pan. Brush with the oil and season with the salt and pepper. Roast until the vegetables are slightly softened, about 15 minutes. Turn the vegetables over and roast until they are tender, about 15 minutes more.

3. While the vegetables roast, make the hummus: Combine the chickpeas, tahini, lemon juice, oil, 2 tablespoons water, and salt in a food processor. Process, occasionally scraping the sides of the work bowl, until the mixture is smooth and fluffy. (If the hummus seems too thick, gradually add 1 to 2 tablespoons more water.)

4. Place the rolls, cut side down, directly on the oven rack and toast until they are lightly golden, 3 to 4 minutes.

5. To serve, spread the hummus over the cut sides of the bottom halves of the rolls. Layer the vegetables over the hummus and close the sandwiches.

## SISTERHOOD OF THE TRAVELING SANDWICHES

These sandwiches travel well and are just as good—if not better—made a day ahead. The hummus soaks into the bread just enough to flavor it but not so much that the entire roll gets soggy. The key is to wrap the sandwiches individually and fairly tightly in plenty of plastic wrap and keep them refrigerated. We have made a slew of these in advance and served them, cut into 2-inch-wide strips, at a casual barbecue. Our vegetarian friends make a meal of them while the carnivores eat one or two as a side dish.

Pass it along. . . .

# RED BEAN AND VEGETABLE BURRITOS WITH PICO DE GALLO

1 (10-ounce) bag frozen brown rice

### PICO DE GALLO

¼ cup chopped onion

3 plum tomatoes (about 1 pound), seeded and chopped (about 1½ cups)

1 jalapeño pepper, finely chopped

2 tablespoons chopped fresh cilantro

1 tablespoon fresh lime juice

¼ teaspoon salt

---

1 tablespoon olive oil

¾ cup chopped onion

1 medium zucchini (about 10 ounces), trimmed and cut into ½-inch cubes (about 1½ cups)

1 cup fresh or frozen corn kernels

2 teaspoons chili powder

1 (15-ounce) can low-sodium red kidney beans, drained

½ teaspoon salt

4 (8-inch) flour tortillas

¾ cup shredded sharp Cheddar cheese, divided

SKILLET
BEANS

If we were to pick a plant-based meal to feed avowed carnivores, this hearty burrito would be it. We like to start by making the pico de gallo and letting the flavors of the fresh tomato topping bloom while we prepare the filling. (In the summer, we make this same pico de gallo with just-picked ripe tomatoes to serve with chips.) The filling is a very satisfying combination of sweet crunch from the corn and zucchini and soft, earthy rice and beans.

You can make the filling ahead; it keeps well in the refrigerator for a couple of days. But don't put it in the tortillas until you are ready to bake and eat them or they will get soggy.

**MAKES 4 SERVINGS**

1. Position a rack in the center of the oven without any racks above it. Preheat the oven to 350°F. Cut 4 (12-inch) lengths of foil and set aside.

2. Microwave the rice according to package directions and transfer it to a bowl.

3. Make the pico de gallo: Combine the onion, tomatoes, jalapeño, cilantro, lime juice, and salt in a bowl.

4. Heat the oil in a large skillet over medium-high heat. Add the onion and cook, stirring occasionally, until slightly softened, 3 to 4 minutes. Add the zucchini, corn, and chili powder and cook, stirring occasionally, until the vegetables are tender, 5 to 6 minutes. Stir in the beans, rice, and salt and cook until heated through, 1 to 2 minutes.

5. Warm the tortillas in the microwave on high for 30 seconds to make them more pliable. Stack them on a plate and cover with a damp paper towel.

6. Coat the top of each foil sheet with cooking spray. Working with one at a time, place a tortilla flat in the center. Spoon one-quarter of the bean mixture in a log shape down the center, leaving about a 1½-inch border clear at the top and bottom. Top the beans with 2 tablespoons of the Cheddar. Fold the top and bottom edges of the

tortilla in toward the center and roll the sides closed to completely encase the filling. Place the burrito, seam side down, in the center of the foil and spoon 2 tablespoons of the pico de gallo on top. Sprinkle with 1 tablespoon of the Cheddar. Bring the two sides of the foil up toward the center, well above the burrito, and crimp it closed. Crimp or fold the sides closed as well, forming a package that looks like a purse. (You are trying to avoid having the foil touch the cheese on top.) Repeat to make three more burrito packets.

7. Place the packets on the oven rack and bake until the burritos are heated through and the cheese is melted, about 20 minutes.

8. Serve with the remaining pico de gallo.

# FIG, ASPARAGUS, AND GOAT CHEESE GALETTE

GREEN SALAD WITH DIJON-BALSAMIC VINAIGRETTE

¾ cup part-skim ricotta cheese

4 ounces goat cheese (chèvre style), softened

1 teaspoon chopped fresh thyme

½ teaspoon salt, divided

12 ounces asparagus, trimmed and cut into 1½-inch lengths

8 fresh figs (about 10 ounces), quartered

1 tablespoon honey

2 teaspoons extra virgin olive oil

Pie Crust Dough (recipe follows)

All-purpose flour, for dusting

1 large egg, lightly beaten

SHEET PAN
CHEESE

Oh, this pretty thing! Its beauty is truly not just skin deep—it tastes every bit as good as it looks. And we aren't talking about some high-maintenance diva here; as long as we have pie crust dough on hand, we can do all the prep to whip up this galette in less than 10 minutes. It bakes for about 35 minutes and must rest at least 5 before you slice it. With a salad and a glass of wine, this galette makes a truly lovely light meal.

Okay, let's talk about pie crust dough. David's recipe for the perfect dough is below. Here's our rule of thumb: *always make a double batch*. Wrap one batch in several layers of plastic wrap and place it in a freezer-worthy plastic bag, where it will keep well for 6 months. Or wrap it well and keep it in the refrigerator for up to about 2 weeks. You'll be so glad you did.

On the other hand, don't let the idea of making your own dough keep you from this galette. The Pillsbury refrigerated crusts work really well (roll it out to a 13-inch diameter). Either way, you will end up with a delicious, knock-your-socks-off dinner.

**MAKES 4 SERVINGS**

1. Preheat the oven to 400°F. Coat a sheet pan with cooking spray.
2. Combine the ricotta cheese, goat cheese, thyme, and ¼ teaspoon of the salt in a bowl. Combine the asparagus, figs, honey, oil, and remaining ¼ teaspoon salt in a separate bowl.
3. Roll the dough out to a 13-inch-diameter round on a lightly floured surface. Transfer to the sheet pan (the edges will hang off the sides of the pan).
4. Spread the cheese mixture over the dough leaving a 2-inch border all the way around. Arrange the asparagus and figs over the cheese. Fold the edges of the crust up and over the filling, pleating them as you go. Brush the dough with some of the beaten egg to coat.
5. Bake until the crust is golden and the filling is bubbling, 33 to 35 minutes. Let the galette cool for 5 minutes before cutting into wedges.

# PIE CRUST DOUGH

1½ cups all-purpose flour

½ teaspoon salt

4 tablespoons (½ stick) cold unsalted butter, cut into small pieces

4 tablespoons vegetable shortening, chilled

1 teaspoon cider vinegar

4 to 5 tablespoons cold water

Combine the flour and salt in a medium bowl. Add the butter and shortening and use a pastry blender or two forks to cut them into the flour mixture until it resembles coarse crumbs. Add the vinegar and water, 1 tablespoon at a time, stirring with a fork until a rough dough forms. Knead the dough in the bowl once or twice to bring it together. Press it into a 4-inch-diameter disk. Wrap in plastic wrap and freeze for 20 minutes before rolling out for a crust.

**NOTE**: *To make the dough in the food processor, follow the directions above but take care that you don't overwork the dough. Pulse—don't run the machine—until the dough forms a ball. Be sure to stop and scrape down the sides several times in between pulses.*

# BAKED RISOTTO WITH SHIITAKES AND ASPARAGUS

3 tablespoons olive oil, divided

8 ounces shiitake mushrooms, stems discarded and caps cut into ¼-inch-wide strips

1 teaspoon salt, divided

½ teaspoon ground black pepper, divided

12 ounces asparagus, trimmed and cut into 1½-inch lengths

½ cup drained oil-packed sun-dried tomatoes, sliced

1 medium onion, chopped (about 1 cup)

3 garlic cloves, minced

1 teaspoon chopped fresh thyme or ¼ teaspoon dried

1 cup Arborio rice

½ cup dry white wine, such as Sauvignon Blanc

3 cups unsalted vegetable broth

½ cup grated Pecorino Romano cheese

½ cup whole-milk ricotta cheese

SKILLET
CHEESE

We were certain that the Italian cooking gods would smite us for trying to cook risotto in the oven . . . and we were also skeptical that we could get the desired al dente grains and creaminess if we didn't follow the revered method of slowly ladling hot broth into the rice while constantly stirring.

We have long held that risotto is better cooked in a skillet than a deep saucepan, because the heat cooks the rice more evenly. But we also erroneously believed that the constant stirring caused the starches to slough off the exterior of the rice and form the lovely creamy foundation. It turns out the starches develop with no stirring at all. We get exactly the same wonderful, creamy, and slightly al dente risotto from letting it bake unattended!

We've chosen to add asparagus and shiitakes to our risotto. You can also use small chunks of lobster or crab, chicken, or a variety of other meats. Whatever you'd like in your risotto, just cook it in the skillet first and stir it in at the end: the heat of the rice will warm it through.

**MAKES 4 SERVINGS**

1. Preheat the oven to 400°F.
2. Heat 1 tablespoon of the oil in a large ovenproof skillet over medium-high heat. Add the shiitakes, ¼ teaspoon of the salt, and ⅛ teaspoon of the pepper and cook, stirring occasionally, until the mushrooms are tender and browned, 6 to 7 minutes. Transfer to a large bowl.
3. Heat 1 tablespoon of the oil in the skillet over medium-high heat. Stir in the asparagus, ¼ teaspoon of the salt, and ⅛ teaspoon of the pepper and cook until the asparagus is bright green, stirring often, about 2 minutes. Add the sun-dried tomatoes and cook for 1 minute. Transfer to the bowl with the mushrooms.
4. Reduce the heat to medium, add the remaining 1 tablespoon oil, the onion, garlic, and thyme and cook until the onion is slightly softened, 2 to 3 minutes. Add the rice and cook, stirring, for 1 minute.

Add the wine and cook until it is nearly absorbed, about 1 minute. Add the broth and the remaining ½ teaspoon salt and ¼ teaspoon pepper. Increase the heat to medium-high and bring to a simmer. Cover the skillet, transfer to the oven, and bake until the liquid is absorbed and the rice is tender, 20 to 22 minutes.

5. Stir in the reserved vegetables, the Romano, and ricotta.

# SICILIAN SQUASH BOWLS WITH LENTILS

2 acorn squash (about 1½ pounds each), halved lengthwise and seeded

2 tablespoons olive oil, divided

1 medium onion, chopped (about 1 cup)

1 large zucchini (about 12 ounces), cut into ½-inch dice (about 1¾ cups)

½ teaspoon salt, divided

¼ teaspoon ground black pepper, divided

1 (15-ounce) can lentils, drained and rinsed

¾ cup canned tomato sauce

⅓ cup golden raisins

1 tablespoon drained nonpareil capers

½ teaspoon dried oregano

½ teaspoon garlic powder

¼ teaspoon ground cumin

⅓ cup shredded Parmesan cheese

**SHEET PAN**
LENTILS

This dish is at its most compelling when you can scoop up a little of the velvety roasted squash and the tomatoey filling of earthy lentils, sweet raisins, and a briny caper in one forkful.

The nutty-sweet acorn squash is both the vessel for and the focal point of this autumnal meatless meal. To make it a side dish for a gathering (Thanksgiving!), replace the lentils with a handful of toasted walnuts. Either way, it can be made ahead and reheated in the oven or microwave. In fact, my favorite part may be the leftovers, which taste every bit as good and make a perfectly satisfying and healthful lunch.

**MAKES 4 SERVINGS**

1. Preheat the oven to 400°F. Coat a sheet pan with cooking spray.
2. Cut a thin slice from the bottom (skin side) of each acorn squash half so that they sit flat. Brush the cavity (flesh) surfaces with 1 tablespoon of the oil. Place the squash, cavity side down, on the pan and bake for 30 minutes.
3. Meanwhile, combine the onion, zucchini, remaining 1 tablespoon oil, ¼ teaspoon of the salt, and ⅛ teaspoon of the pepper in a bowl.
4. Add the onion and zucchini to the sheet pan and cook until the acorn squash is fork-tender but holds its shape and the onion and zucchini are tender, 18 to 20 minutes more. Transfer the onion and zucchini to a large bowl and add the lentils, tomato sauce, raisins, capers, oregano, garlic powder, cumin, and the remaining ¼ teaspoon salt and ⅛ teaspoon pepper. Stir to combine.
5. Flip the acorn squash over so the cavity is facing up. Spoon the lentil mixture into the squash and bake until the filling is hot and the squash is very tender, 10 to 12 minutes. Sprinkle with the Parmesan cheese.

# 5

# BONUS TREATS

While the recipes in this chapter are not for dinner, we would like to point out that there are times desserts and snacks can also swoop in and save our days, just as a one-pan meal can. (What better way to treat heartbreak than with a nice big piece of warm bread pudding topped with ice cream!) For that reason, and because we couldn't resist sharing our family favorites with you, we've included these very simple sheet-pan and skillet treats.

# LEMON CORNMEAL POUND CAKE (TWO WAYS)

STRAWBERRY POUND CAKE + PLUM POUND CAKE

3 sticks (12 ounces) unsalted butter, softened, plus more for the pan

2½ cups all-purpose flour, plus more for dusting the pan

½ cup cornmeal (fine to medium grind)

1½ teaspoons baking powder

½ teaspoon baking soda

½ teaspoon salt

1½ cups plus 1 tablespoon sugar, divided

8 large eggs

¾ cup low-fat buttermilk

1 tablespoon grated lemon zest

¼ cup fresh lemon juice

1 pound strawberries, hulled and quartered

SKILLET
DESSERT

Our basic skillet pound cake works with endless variations. In the spring we love the version with strawberries. In the summer we might use plums or other stone fruit and in the winter apples or pears. We also make this pound cake with no fruit at all and serve it with fruit compote spooned over the top.

MAKES 12 TO 16 SERVINGS

1. Preheat the oven to 350°F. Butter a large skillet and dust it with flour to coat.
2. Combine the flour, cornmeal, baking powder, baking soda, and salt in a bowl. Combine the butter and 1½ cups of the sugar in the bowl of an electric mixer and beat on high speed until light and fluffy, 2 to 3 minutes. With the mixer on medium, beat in the eggs one at a time, stopping to scrape down the bowl after each addition. Beat in the buttermilk, lemon zest, and lemon juice. Turn the mixer to low speed and beat in the flour mixture until the flour is just moistened.
3. Combine the strawberries with the remaining 1 tablespoon sugar.
4. Pour half of the batter into the prepared pan. Spoon the strawberries over the batter in an even layer. Top with the remaining batter.
5. Bake until a wooden pick inserted into the center of the cake comes out clean, 52 to 54 minutes. Let the cake cool in the pan for 30 minutes.

## VARIATION: LEMON PLUM CORNMEAL POUND CAKE

- Omit the strawberries.

- Pit and thinly slice 1 pound plums.

- Pour all the batter into the prepared pan. Arrange the plum slices in an overlapping spiral, working from the center out to the edges of the pan. Sprinkle the plums with the remaining 1 tablespoon sugar. Bake according to step 5 above.

# DOUBLE STREUSEL SKILLET COFFEE CAKE

## STREUSEL

**6 tablespoons (¾ stick) unsalted butter, softened, plus more for the skillet**

**1 cup lightly packed light brown sugar**

**½ cup old-fashioned rolled oats**

**½ cup all-purpose flour**

**1 cup walnuts, chopped**

**1 tablespoon ground cinnamon**

**¼ teaspoon salt**

## CAKE

**1½ sticks (6 ounces) unsalted butter, softened**

**1⅔ cups granulated sugar**

**3 large eggs, lightly beaten**

**1 cup sour cream**

**½ cup low-fat buttermilk**

**1 tablespoon pure vanilla extract**

**3 cups all-purpose flour**

**1½ teaspoons baking powder**

**½ teaspoon baking soda**

**½ teaspoon salt**

SKILLET
DESSERT

Streusel in the middle and streusel on top: yep, we think that is as it should be! This is the cake we make to bring to someone who just moved into their new home, or someone who is blue; it is the cake we make to celebrate hanging out with friends on a Sunday morning or a visitor coming over for an afternoon chat. This is the cake we make anytime we want an easy, universally beloved, no-fail dessert.

Pecans make a great, slightly sweeter stand-in for the walnuts.

**MAKES 12 TO 16 SERVINGS**

1. Preheat the oven to 350°F. Generously butter the bottom and sides of a large skillet.

2. Make the streusel: Combine the brown sugar, oats, flour, walnuts, cinnamon, and salt in a bowl. Add the 6 tablespoons butter and rub it into the sugar mixture with your fingertips until it is well combined and clumps form when pressed together.

3. Make the cake: Combine the butter and granulated sugar in the bowl of an electric mixer and beat on high speed until light and fluffy, 2 to 3 minutes. Whisk together the eggs, sour cream, buttermilk, and vanilla in a separate bowl; add to the sugar mixture and beat on medium speed, stopping occasionally to scrape down the sides of the bowl. Combine the flour, baking powder, baking soda, and salt in a separate bowl. Add the flour mixture to the sugar mixture and beat on low speed until the flour is just moistened, 1 to 2 minutes.

4. Spread half of the batter in the prepared skillet. Top with one-third of the streusel mixture in an even layer. Spread the remaining batter over the streusel. Sprinkle with the remaining streusel.

5. Bake, rotating the pan every 15 minutes, until the streusel is golden brown and a wooden toothpick inserted into the center of the cake comes out clean, 50 to 55 minutes. Let the cake cool for at least 20 minutes.

# ROAST PEARS WITH HONEYED BALSAMIC PECANS

1 cup pecans, coarsely chopped

4 medium Bosc pears (about 2 pounds)

8 tablespoons honey, divided

1 tablespoon balsamic vinegar

1 tablespoon unsalted butter

Pinch of ground cardamom

**SHEET PAN**
DESSERT

Roasting pears intensifies their flavor and brings out their natural sugars. The nut topping, with its slightly acidic balance, elevates the simple baked pears into a party-worthy treat. By all means, double the topping and serve the pears with a scoop of vanilla ice cream, with more of the honey-nut mixture spooned over the top.

**MAKES 8 SERVINGS**

1. Preheat the oven to 425°F.
2. Spread the pecans on a sheet pan and bake until lightly toasted, about 5 minutes. Transfer to a bowl.
3. Coat the sheet pan with cooking spray.
4. Cut each pear in half lengthwise, leaving the stem attached to one half when possible (because it looks nice). Use a melon baller to scoop out the core. (If one or more of the halves is too lopsided, cut a sliver off the bottom to help it sit flat.) Place the pears, cavity side down, on the pan and roast for 15 minutes.
5. Meanwhile, combine 6 tablespoons of the honey and the vinegar in a small bowl and stir until the honey is thinned.
6. Turn the pears over so the cavity side faces up and brush lightly with some of the honey-balsamic mixture. Roast until the pears are fork-tender and slightly browned on the edges, about 15 minutes more.
7. Meanwhile, melt the butter in a microwave-safe bowl. Stir in the pecans, cardamom, remaining 2 tablespoons honey, and remaining honey-balsamic mixture.
8. Spoon the nut mixture over the pears. Serve warm or at room temperature.

# PEACH, GRAPE, AND BLUEBERRY CRISP

## TOPPING

**6 tablespoons (¾ stick) unsalted butter, cut into small pieces, plus more for the skillet**

**1 cup all-purpose flour**

**¾ cup old-fashioned rolled oats**

**⅔ cup lightly packed light brown sugar**

**½ cup pecans, chopped**

**¼ teaspoon salt**

## FILLING

**2 pounds peaches (about 7), pitted and cut into ½-inch-thick wedges**

**30 ounces (about 5 cups or 2½ pints) fresh or frozen thawed blueberries**

**2 cups seedless green grapes (about 12 ounces), halved**

**1 cup granulated sugar**

**½ teaspoon almond extract**

**⅓ cup all-purpose flour**

SKILLET
DESSERT

We're not really sure why grapes so rarely make an appearance in fruit crisps, but they add wonderful flavor and texture.

We sometimes make a double batch of the topping and keep it in the freezer, which makes short work of whipping up a crisp.

**MAKES 10 TO 12 SERVINGS**

1. Preheat the oven to 375°F. Lightly butter a large skillet.
2. Make the topping: Combine the flour, oats, brown sugar, pecans, and salt in a medium bowl. Add the 6 tablespoons butter and rub it into the sugar mixture with your fingertips until it is well combined and clumps form when pressed together.
3. Make the filling: Toss the peaches, blueberries, grapes, granulated sugar, and almond extract in a large bowl. Add the flour and toss well to coat. Transfer the mixture to the prepared skillet and sprinkle evenly with the topping mixture.
4. Bake, rotating the skillet occasionally, until the filling is thick and bubbling and the topping is lightly browned, 65 to 70 minutes. (If the topping is browning too quickly, loosely cover the crisp with a sheet of foil.) Let cool for at least 20 minutes before serving.

# SKILLET CINNAMON BUNS

**¾ cup warm buttermilk (100° to 105°F)**

**3 tablespoons granulated sugar**

**1 (0.75-ounce) packet active dry yeast**

**2 large eggs**

**½ teaspoon salt**

**2¾ to 3 cups all-purpose flour**

**4 tablespoons (½ stick) unsalted butter, softened, plus more for the skillet**

**Canola oil, for the bowl**

FILLING

**1 cup lightly packed dark brown sugar**

**1½ teaspoons ground cinnamon**

**3 tablespoons unsalted butter, softened**

GLAZE

**1 cup confectioners' sugar**

**2 tablespoons buttermilk**

**2 teaspoons unsalted butter, melted**

**½ teaspoon pure vanilla extract**

SKILLET
BRUNCH

Throw out every aromatherapy candle you own—baking cinnamon buns makes the ultimate feel-good scent. But it's not just the aroma—you can't help but feel good when you eat one of these soft, fluffy buns spiraled around brown sugar–cinnamon filling and topped with sweet buttermilk glaze.

*Don't fear the yeast.* We have step-by-step instructions below, so if you've never worked with yeast before, this is your well-guided opportunity. You'll see the buns are not hard to make, although they are time consuming. But they are so, so, so worth it.

If you want to serve these for brunch, form them in the skillet the night before, then take them out to sit at room temperature for 45 minutes before baking.

**MAKES 16 SERVINGS**

1.  Make the dough: Be sure your buttermilk is at 100° to 105°F—if it is too hot, it can kill the yeast, and if it is too cold (below 90°F), the dough will rise too slowly. Whisk the buttermilk, sugar, and yeast in the bowl of an electric mixer and let it stand until frothy, about 5 minutes. Use the paddle attachment on medium-high speed to beat in the eggs and salt.

2.  Change to the dough hook. Add 2¾ cups of the flour and mix on medium speed until a smooth dough forms, 3 to 4 minutes. (The dough starts out as a lumpy mess but will be smooth and slightly tacky when it is ready.) Reduce the speed to medium-low and add the butter and enough of the remaining flour, 1 tablespoon at a time, so that the dough is not sticky but smooth and soft. Transfer to a lightly oiled bowl, cover with plastic wrap, and let rise in a somewhat warm place until doubled in bulk, 1 to 1½ hours.

3.  Meanwhile, cut a round out of parchment paper that is about 2 inches wider than the bottom of your skillet. Place it in the skillet, pressing it into the bottom of the pan so it goes about 1 inch up the sides. Brush the parchment with a little softened butter.

4.  While the dough rises, make the filling: Combine the brown sugar and cinnamon in a bowl and mix well.

5.  Press the dough down in the bowl, then turn it out onto a lightly floured surface. Knead it two or three times with the heels of your

hands, then roll it out with a lightly floured rolling pin to a 20 x 12-inch rectangle. Spread the top of the dough with the 3 tablespoons softened butter; sprinkle the filling mixture evenly over the butter.

6. Starting with one long edge, tightly roll up the dough jelly-roll style. Slice the log into 16 even pieces. Arrange the buns, cut side facing up, in a single layer in the skillet. Cover the pan with plastic wrap and let the buns rise for 30 minutes. (If you are preparing them in advance, let them rise 30 minutes at room temperature before refrigerating.)

7. Preheat the oven to 350°F.

8. Remove the plastic wrap and bake until the buns are browned and cooked through, 25 to 27 minutes. Let the buns cool at least 20 minutes.

9. Meanwhile, make the glaze: Combine the confectioners' sugar, buttermilk, melted butter, and vanilla in a bowl and mix until smooth. Drizzle the glaze over the buns with a spoon and let it set for at least 10 minutes before serving.

# SWEET AND SPICY NUTS

1 large egg white

1 pound raw nuts (pecans, skin-on almonds, or walnuts)

⅔ cup sugar

1½ teaspoons ground cumin

1½ teaspoons salt

1 teaspoon chipotle chile powder

¾ teaspoon ground cinnamon

½ teaspoon ground allspice

SHEET PAN
SNACK

It wouldn't be the holidays without the sweet and savory aroma of batch upon batch of these nuts wafting from the oven. We bottle up the cooled nuts in mason jars, tie them up with pretty ribbons, and send them out to colleagues, friends, and family.

But these nuts are not just for the holidays. They freeze really well (we store them in zip-top plastic bags), and when we are going to friends' homes for dinner or want to show someone gratitude, we make up a jar.

We've often wondered if after all these years, people might be bored with receiving the same food treat from us time and again. We got our answer last year when a young colleague wrote us that she was excited to be on our list of nut recipients and finally get her own jar. Apparently her boss had not been a good sharer.

MAKES 2½ CUPS

1. Preheat the oven to 275°F.
2. Combine the egg white and 1 tablespoon water in a large bowl and beat with a whisk until frothy. Add the nuts and toss well to coat. Transfer the nuts to a colander and let drain for 10 minutes.
3. Meanwhile, in a small bowl, combine the sugar, cumin, salt, chipotle powder, cinnamon, and allspice. Pour the mixture into a large plastic bag, add the nuts, and shake until they are well coated with the sugar mixture.
4. Spread the nuts in an even layer on a sheet pan and bake for 15 minutes. Remove from the oven and stir. Reduce the oven temperature to 250°F and bake, stirring every 15 minutes, until the coating on the nuts is dry, 45 to 55 minutes.
5. Remove from the oven, stir the nuts well, and let them cool completely, about 25 minutes. (The nuts crisp as they cool.) Store in an airtight container.

# VARIATIONS: SWEET AND SPICED NUTS

We make many variations of spiced nuts—some are sweet and others more savory. We toss them in salads, serve them as pre-dinner nibbles, sprinkle them on ice cream, eat them as snacks . . . well, you get the idea. Here are a few of our favorites:

### SAVORY
**Almonds/pecans**
**⅓ cup sugar**
**1 tablespoon salt**
**2 teaspoons paprika**
**1 teaspoon ground cumin**
**1 teaspoon ground coriander**
**1 teaspoon garlic powder**
**⅛ teaspoon cayenne**

### CURRIED
**Almonds/walnuts**
**½ cup sugar**
**1 tablespoon curry powder**
**1 teaspoon ground cumin**
**½ teaspoon ground coriander**
**2 teaspoons salt**
**¼ teaspoon cayenne**

### SMOKY
**Almonds/walnuts**
**⅓ cup sugar**
**2 teaspoons salt**
**2 teaspoons smoked paprika**
**1 teaspoon chili powder**
**1 teaspoon ground coriander**
**½ teaspoon black pepper**

# APPLE-WALNUT BREAD PUDDING

4 large eggs

2½ cups milk

½ cup sugar

¾ cup pure maple syrup, divided

1 teaspoon pure vanilla extract

1 pound country-style white or sourdough bread, cut into 1-inch chunks (about 10 cups)

2 Golden Delicious apples, peeled, cored, and cut into ½-inch dice (about 2½ cups)

½ cup walnuts, chopped

Vanilla ice cream, for serving (optional)

SHEET PAN
DESSERT

Making bread pudding in a sheet pan has the delicious advantage of having more crispy bits around the edges than one baked in the traditional pan. We also love the larger, flatter serving pieces, which feel like we are getting bigger portions even when we're not.

Make this bread pudding your own: Use different bread, such as cinnamon or challah/brioche. You can use any milk you like to keep on hand, from fat-free to whole. Leave out the fruit entirely, or try pears, halved grapes, strawberries, blueberries, or any other fruit instead. Feel free to substitute other nuts, including pecans and sliced or slivered almonds. The variations are endless: we have made a tropical version with mango in place of apples, plus macadamia nuts and toasted coconut.

### MAKES 8 SERVINGS

1. Preheat the oven to 375°F. Coat a sheet pan with cooking spray.
2. Whisk the eggs, milk, sugar, ¼ cup of the maple syrup, and the vanilla in a large bowl. Add the bread and stir to coat. Let the mixture stand at least 5 minutes (or overnight in the refrigerator) so the bread soaks up the liquid. Fold in the apples and walnuts.
3. Arrange the bread mixture in an even layer on the sheet pan. Pour any liquid remaining in the bowl over the bread.
4. Bake until the bread is puffed, lightly browned, and crisp on top and the custard is set, 34 to 35 minutes. Let stand 5 minutes before cutting.
5. Drizzle each serving with the remaining maple syrup. (You can warm it first in the microwave if you like.) Serve with ice cream, if desired.

# MAPLE-PECAN GRANOLA

**4 cups old-fashioned rolled oats**

**1½ cups pecans, roughly chopped**

**⅓ cup sesame seeds**

**1 teaspoon ground cinnamon**

**¼ teaspoon ground allspice**

**¼ teaspoon salt**

**¾ cup pure maple syrup**

**⅓ cup canola oil**

**1 teaspoon pure vanilla extract**

**⅔ cup golden raisins**

**⅓ cup dried cranberries**

SHEET PAN
BREAKFAST AND SNACK

Granola is really rewarding to make. For one thing, it tastes so good—on yogurt in the morning, as a snack in the afternoon, or over ice cream for dessert. One batch also lasts a while—and it makes a great host or thank-you gift. We're partial to this maple-pecan version because it is not overly sweet, and the maple gives it an earthy, almost smoky flavor. (Also, David loves all things maple.)

**MAKES 7 CUPS**

1.  Preheat the oven to 300°F. Coat a large sheet pan with cooking spray.
2.  Combine the oats, pecans, sesame seeds, cinnamon, allspice, and salt in a large bowl. Combine the maple syrup, oil, and vanilla in a separate bowl. Add the maple-syrup mixture to the oat mixture and stir well to combine. Spread the mixture in an even layer on the sheet pan.
3.  Bake, stirring every 10 minutes, until the oats are lightly browned, 40 to 45 minutes. Remove from the oven and stir in the raisins and cranberries. Cool completely and store in an airtight container.

# RECIPES BY CATEGORY

# UNIVERSAL CONVERSION CHART

## OVEN TEMPERATURE EQUIVALENTS

250°F = 120°C          350°F = 180°C          450°F = 230°C

275°F = 135°C          375°F = 190°C          475°F = 240°C

300°F = 150°C          400°F = 200°C          500°F = 260°C

325°F = 160°C          425°F = 220°C

## MEASUREMENT EQUIVALENTS

Measurements should always be level unless directed otherwise.

⅛ teaspoon = 0.5 mL

¼ teaspoon = 1 mL

½ teaspoon = 2 mL

1 teaspoon = 5 mL

1 tablespoon = 3 teaspoons = ½ fluid ounce = 15 mL

2 tablespoons = ⅛ cup = 1 fluid ounce = 30 mL

4 tablespoons = ¼ cup = 2 fluid ounces = 60 mL

5⅓ tablespoons = ⅓ cup = 3 fluid ounces = 80 mL

8 tablespoons = ½ cup = 4 fluid ounces = 120 mL

10⅔ tablespoons = ⅔ cup = 5 fluid ounces = 160 mL

12 tablespoons = ¾ cup = 6 fluid ounces = 180 mL

16 tablespoons = 1 cup = 8 fluid ounces = 240 mL

# ACKNOWLEDGMENTS

This book came about thanks to a whole village of heroes.

Our agent, Sharon Bowers, championed this book to the editor of editors: the astoundingly patient, ever-responsive Cassie Jones.

When it comes to friends, we hit the jackpot. Special thanks to Laurie, David, Vivien, Andy, Amy, and Tracy for your dedicated commitment to taste-testing—and giving our life balance. Barb and Cynth: you are in our hearts as friends as much as sisters.

A conversation at lunch one day with our very smart friend Cathy Schreiber made us realize this was the book we wanted to write. Thank you, Cathy, for (among much else) your insight and thoughtfulness.

Brittany Lima, your savvy, integrity, and trust mean the world to us. You are the whole package and we adore you.

Ruby, our beloved kitchen assistant: your *"muy rico!"* after tasting means more to us than you will ever know.

The invaluable team at William Morrow, including Rachel Meyers, Kara Zauberman, Renata De Oliveira, Tavia Kowalchuk, Ryan Cury, Anwesha Basu, Anna Brower, and Kate Slate: thank you!

Thank you to the talented Amy Finkel and Matt Taylor-Gross: you both made standing on the other side of the camera fun. And thanks to Grace Young: in addition to being a wonderful friend, your keen eye got us off on the right path.

Finally: Hope, you add buckets of joy to our lives.

# INDEX

NOTE: Page references in *italics* refer to photos.